EXIT HOUSE

EXIT HOUSE

JO ROMAN

Seaview **Books**

NEW YORK

Library of Congress Cataloging in Publication Data

Roman, Jo.
    Exit house.

        1. Roman, Jo.   2. Suicide—Biography.   I. Title.
HV6545.R62   362.2   80-52420
ISBN 0-87223-649-8

Design by Tere LoPrete

DEDICATED

Compassionately, to anyone who finds life too difficult or not worth living.

Encouragingly, to anyone who would try to create a good completion of a life-canvas.

Appreciatively, to those who, drawn into my orbit, dared aid me; some laboriously, some courageously, some uneasily, all lovingly.

Monumentally, to Mel, who braved walking with me the whole way.

Ultimately, for everyone who would liberate humankind from ignorance and blinding belief systems.

Especially, for the young.

The wish to leave life is profoundly different from the wish to destroy it.

—Jo ROMAN

Contents

Foreword

by Mel Roman

Not all of us, among family and friends, easily accepted Jo's advocacy of rational suicide when it was still theoretical, let alone afterward. In my case, the time between intellectual acceptance and emotional understanding was long and agonizing. I had to grapple with feelings of selfishness and guilt, with issues around respect for the rights of others, with concerns about possible consequences to myself and others. I came to recognize that a significant part of my early resistance and anger derived from my unacknowledged fears of facing death.

During this period, Jo and I talked as most people rarely have the chance to do. In time my acceptance came, out of my love for her and my respect for her independence and integrity. As we came to terms with her impending death, I found I was gaining a better understanding of her life, and of mine as well.

It was important for me to be there for Jo, and with Jo, as we reached out to our family and to the larger family of intimate friends. We never believed that all our discussions and anticipatory grieving would preclude the pain of her death, and it did not—but it helped me recover from the loss. Painful as it was, the experience has changed and enriched me, and in this I am not alone. Many who shared some portion of her last months have told me that they have gained deeper insight into the meaning of their lives.

Some people have objected to the political aspect of Jo's suicide, to the fact that it was not done privately. Jo was an intensely private person, but she was also a political one, committed to the struggle for human rights. She was outraged by the existing situation, whereby life can be imposed on those who no longer desire it. It was consistent with our philosophy and past practice to take a public stand on issues of social and political importance.

Though we were aware of the potentially damaging consequences for me and perhaps other members of the family, we were finally determined to bring this issue to public attention, and asked our family and friends to support our efforts. In December of 1978, after a sudden and unexpected change in her physical condition, Jo worried that she might be too ill to finish her book, and we decided to videotape a weekend of discussions with family and friends. A close friend arranged for the videotaping, and the tapes have been edited into a documentary that illuminates Jo's position, her passionate convictions, her commitment to what she believed to be the ultimate human right. Happily, it also reveals Jo's fine sense of humor, her courage, and her generosity.

The last week of Jo's life was devoted to us. We talked, just the two of us, marathon talking. And we met with members of the family and close friends. The final weekend was for finishing her "life sculpture" and for us to say good-bye. That time was rich with tears and laughter. It was extraordinary that anyone could be so creative and alive, just days and hours before her death, by her own choice; and I think it is important to say that Jo was fully resolved, and totally unafraid. I do not think I could have tolerated it if I had seen any fear or ambivalence in her eyes, and there was none.

She was striving, as I imagine most people do in the face of death, to understand the meaning of her life, and she was doing it in her particular, visual way, through the life sculpture. We worked on it until early in the morning of the last day of her life.

Finally Jo said that was it; we stopped work on the sculpture, realizing that nothing is ever quite finished, completely realized, totally understood, and perhaps that's the way life has to be.

Jo lived every moment fully to the last, and died peacefully in her sleep, as she had wished. I believe her decision and resolve were heroic, and also generous beyond exaggeration. She hoped her legacy would help others to live fully and die well. It is a hope shared by all who knew and loved her.

A LETTER
FROM
JO ROMAN

The following letter was mailed to three hundred dred friends and family members on the day of her death, June 10, 1979.

FROM MARY JO
SUNSHINE
CLODFELTER
WADE
CARO
ROMAN
WITH LOVE

By the time you read these lines I WILL HAVE GENTLY ENDED MY LIFE on the date of this letter's postmark. This may come as a surprise to some of you—family, friends, and acquaintances—particularly if the circumstances of our relationship haven't enabled me to keep you apprised of the work I've been doing on the subject of suicide. So, for you who are uninformed, let me summarize the view I've evolved.

More than a decade ago I concluded that suicide need not be pathological. Further, that rational suicide makes possible a truly ideal closing of one's life span. Commitment to a rational suicide spares one erosive accelerating investment against unwanted existence.

More important by far than such practical avoidance, however, is the paradoxical life-enriching value of suicide. Life perspectives clouded by the vagaries and fears of open-endedness become crystal clear. Energies are freed.

By 1975 I had made a commitment to end my own life around 1992. I was confident I'd not find it too difficult to refine an exit date as that year approached. My decision impacted forcefully on those close to me, reverberating outward to others.

My conviction is strong. I want to share it with others in order to raise consciousness. Also and importantly, because I am averse to demeaning myself by closeting an act which I believe deserves respect. Nor do I want to shock persons who might take offense out of a failure to appreciate my decision. So, for years I've addressed myself to eliciting understanding within a commonly resistant culture.

From 1975 to 1978 I engaged each of you whom I possibly could in discussion of the complex issues. Gradually some of you began to appreciate and/or share my views and to contribute to my thinking. The more we explored the deeper grew conviction. Plans for my still distant suicide began taking shape.

How fortuitous that we did all that work! When, in March 1978, I discovered I had advanced cancer, our accumulated respect for rational suicide made it possible for me to draw several of you into my confidence. You understood when I advanced my suicide date. You respected the need to hold secret my condition so that my limited time and energy need not be drained by focus on illness.

Nothing was as important as preserving every possible moment with my intimates and freeing time for the work I've most wanted to complete. I could achieve these vital goals only because there had come into existence a circle of people who were ready to accept, assist, and protect my decision to create the best possible ending for my self.

I knew from the outset that I would not subject myself nor those around me to the emotional strains and physical ravages of terminal cancer. Nor would I jeopardize our life quality and resources by devoting my foreshortened life to a search against odds for cures or postponements of my inevitable premature demise. Instead, I would make the best possible calculation of a time frame within which I might count reasonably on being able to function to my satisfaction.

Then, I decided, I would set an exit date and prepare to meet it. I'd aim for my exit date to predate discomfort of intensity which might diminish my chance of CREATING ON MY OWN TERMS THE FINAL STROKE OF MY LIFE'S CANVAS. I'd hope my selected date would be chosen so well and blessed with such luck that I would be feeling very well. I'd want to be able to enjoy and share the day with others. I'd want none of us burdened with unnecessary distress over my emotional and physical state.

I regret to say that for ten precious months I lost substantial amounts of quality and time by submitting to chemotherapy and its debilitation. Ten long wearing months before my medical team was persuaded to let me know I could probably reach my selected exit date without undue risk and without chemotherapy. In effect, for those months they believed they had more right than I to command my life. But, at long last, they did give the information I needed and, so, returned command to me. Thus I was released into a few months of superb quality.

In the interim my close circle joined forces to help me create my death in the most open, comfortable, and meaningful way possible. They protected my writing time so I could rewrite the manuscript I'd been working on across many years. The book's working title is "Exit House." You will be notified when it is published posthumously. And I hope it will open for you NEW POSSIBILITIES OF LIVING MOST FULLY. My circle also gathered to film a weekend of discussing our shared experience so that, eventually, an educational film may result. An additional part of my statement is a life sculpture.

My circle and I have transformed anguish into the sweet sorrow of our grief. We've experienced remarkable highs of enlightenment. My exit marks their launching beyond me.

No treasure of my life—and there are many!—is greater than the growth emerging from the approach to my death. I don't know words to say how profoundly rewarding it is to be spared traditional isolation and imposed will of others. And to find myself so lovingly accompanied to my last breaths.

I can say, however, that I believe time is at hand when consciousness of personal responsibility for the length of one's life span—as well as for its content—will establish RATIONAL SUICIDE AS A BASIC HUMAN RIGHT TO BE GIVEN SOCIETY'S ASSISTANCE AND PROTECTION. Current imposition of life-extending technology when it is unwanted may well serve to enhance awareness.

The difference between killing oneself and bringing one's life to a responsible good end is the very real difference between pathological and rational suicide. Surely rational suicide is a reasonable and potentially creative way to recycle into universal resources a body one is ready to relinquish. I urge each of you to begin as early as possible—for many it may be too late—to contemplate turning the end of your own life span into one timed and shaped to dignify your own life.

Thinking of your surviving me, I imagine some may feel deprived of participation in these last eventful months. If so, I wish you would know I would have preferred our sharing—if only I had been able. I imagine you may experience a wish to respond or to know more than I can say here. Perhaps you will feel frustrated by the absence of ritual and traditional closings. No funeral. No place to send flowers. Please know it is not meant that you should feel stranded. Your feelings matter and should be heard.

Several people have agreed to be available for calls and you'll find, enclosed, means of contact. If you would be interested in considering whether some sort of rational suicide institute might be developed, Mel would welcome your call later in the fall.

Finally, I very much want you to know I'm glad our lives have touched. Together, all touching has merged to make my life more full and beautiful than I dared dream. I HOPE YOU WILL WORK TO SHAPE YOUR OWN LIFE AND TO CREATE A GOOD END TO DIGNIFY IT. THEN, LET PEACE WASH OVER YOU TOO!

1

EXIT HOUSE: A REALITY

It was about 1965 when I began spreading on paper fantasies of an Exit House, an institute to study and help people execute rational suicide. As I discussed and explored the fantasy with others, I became fully convinced that suicide is not *necessarily* pathological. Indeed, it has a truly remarkable potential force as a means of favorably transforming the quality of one's life span. By establishing one's capacity to determine the end of one's own life span on a constructive thoughtful basis—as contrasted with pathological, depressed, or impulsive bases—one then has options which, paradoxically, become life liberating and enriching.

By 1975, at age fifty-eight, I had moved beyond thinking in generalities and had come to grips with my personal option to control the length of my own life span. My relatives customarily lived into their eighties and nineties, dying finally from sheer old age rather than disease. Still, as I had observed them, by the time they reached eighty, their lives were lacking the quality I would want for myself. I concluded that I would rather die in my seventies. But how would I be able to select a time and means? And how would family, friends, society react?

I set a goal for myself: to learn some answers. I wanted to be prepared by my seventieth birthday with ways to select a suitable time to exit before slipping into a dependent state I did not want. I needed to know the best means of exiting and having them available. I wanted to prepare others so that those close to me could be understanding and accepting and need not be penalized.

Besides, being seventy seemed far off and I couldn't imagine wanting to end my life before, say, age seventy-five. That would be 1992. I labeled a file folder "1992" and began making notes. Somehow I understood that even a decade was a terribly short time for the task. Over and over I had heard people say they would not let themselves become decrepit and dependent, and then had watched as they slipped across the line. People became feeble no matter how surrounded they were by friends talking about their strong will to live. Clearly, my task was difficult, needing much time. I did not live in a world which was prepared to hear my wishes with respect. Help was not available should I choose a time when I'd be ready to push myself away from life. If I wanted to be able to end my life comfortably on terms of my own at some distant date, and to do so without creating social disgrace for which my family and friends would be punished, I would have to create a new social environment.

It was fortunate that my reflections and planning started so early, and even more fortunate was the fact that family and friends came around to discuss my audacious notions with me. They were indulgent at first, but gradually they began to peer into their own lives. I say fortunate because in March 1978 my life took a stunning turn. Cancer of the left breast emerged. Later, when I realized the cancer was irreversible, I advanced my exit date to June 10, 1979. I speak so certainly of my exit time because I know I need not and will not subject my family and friends and myself to the ravages of terminal cancer. Many of my friends have helped in evaluating my options and have shared their wisdom and affection. Their participation proves to be the perfect comfort for a shortened life.

As much as I treasure their offsetting my personal anguish in having my life shortened by at least a decade, there is something I treasure even more. The reactions of the sixty or so persons who now know and are participating in my suicide planning—not all intimately connected—serve to confirm what I had suspected.

One: Although for good or thoughtless reasons humankind has developed deep indoctrination to fight for life extension at all costs *regardless* of how a person perceives the quality of her or his life, basically it must be as much a violation of human rights to force life upon an unwilling person as it is to take a person's life. Two: Suicide has always been a human option. In our Western culture, though certainly not all others, it has come to be regarded automatically as an expression of pathology or immorality—even as we invest large portions of our economy in poisoning our food and air and encouraging youngsters to smoke cancer-producing substances; even as we invite people to enter the powerful lethal weapon known as a car and act out self-destructive impulses which end and mangle the lives of others as well as ourselves. Although we attribute suicide to pathology and/or immorality, we fail to see suicide's nonpathological face and moral value. We also fail to see its potential use as a life enricher and liberator. I hope my book will confirm its value for others as much as for those experiencing with me the truth of this eye-opening paradox.

In any event, there is the truth that I am dying.

At first, only my doctor and I knew. My doctor was a

stranger to me, albeit a considerate and gifted one. He waited for me to respond in a traditional, expected way: to call my family, perhaps, or to wail. Certainly those urges nearly overpowered me. I suppose I would have given in to them had not the image of Exit House stood firmly in my mind. It stood solidly and brilliant with new light upon it, dynamically detailed by years of my mind's exploration and surrounded by many more familiar images, more generally accepted alternatives than a rational suicide.

There was the hospital. It was good for diagnostic work but eager to have me turn responsibility for my being over to it; ready to concern itself with lengthening my life span and only secondarily concerned with my life span's *quality*. It was ready to discharge me to a nursing home or hospice whenever its ability to extend my life would be reduced merely to support existence (or when my family's financial resources would be drained).

And there was the nursing home or hospice. One of the very best ones, not the ones which are routine parts of the burgeoning money-making terminal-care industry. I myself saw a home or hospice equipped with the most advanced programs for alleviation of physical pain—perhaps drugs which could send me tripping into some glorious psychedelic mind space. It would be staffed with the most dedicated people whose gratification comes from mastery of their impulses to turn away from the suffering and dying; from learning new techniques to teach to patients and family which will stiffen their upper lips and train their brains to make peace with their terminal agonies; from being inordinately gentle and compassionate, listening and understanding. If I'd want to die their way—and it does seem a better choice than people heretofore have had—I'd indeed be grateful to be taken into their care. And I'm happy for people to have the option of such settings for their life endings. However, with the image of Exit House before me, such alternatives lured me not at all.

But how could suicide be an optional life ending for me in the absence of a real Exit House? First of all, even confronted with the still searing news of my cancer, I felt not at all suicidal. I had impulses to scream and run berserk, but nary an inclination to commit an impulsive suicide. My life's agenda was too full of living and work I wanted to do before I could act to end my life. I sought an Exit House for much more than its spontaneous respect of my right to commit suicide! I wanted the assurance that I would have the best *means* of suicide and assistance, if needed, at whatever moment I would choose to end my life. An Exit House would help me learn from the medical world precisely what they truly believed my medical reality to be, and provide that information in language I could understand clearly and without my having to ferret it out. And Exit House would aid me in coping with people who would gasp at news of my cancer and then—not because they didn't care about me but because they hadn't resolved socially imposed fears of their own dying—cover their recoil from my dying with distancing looks of pity. I would be able to cope with people who would protest and present obstacles to my declared suicidal intent—insisting on translating my declaration as an expression of despondency and refusing to see it as my constructive way of liberating the remainder of my life. And an Exit House would help people who would suffer at the thought of my committing suicide—blaming themselves for not being able to make me want to live through an unwanted time of life, wondering whether my sanity was at stake.

I wanted to hear people—my fellow human beings, an Exit House staff, my family, friends, and others—say to me: Jo, what a shock to have your life shortened! Let us help you determine what probable length your new life span can be. And what choices you have for its contents. We want to help you make it as fully worth living as possible. We don't want you to suffer unnecessarily— either physically or emotionally. If you want not to subject yourself and us to your stage of terminal cancer, or for that matter to your having to live any other sort of unwanted existence, please know that we don't want you to be forced to live against your will. Please know *we will help you find the best moment and means of ending your life*. And if suicide is your choice, let us help you die forthrightly and with self-respect. Above all, until your death, let us together make our shared living as comfortable and creative as possible.

I looked about me last March 1978, standing alone, longing for an Exit House, seeing none except in my imagination, listening for the words I wanted to hear and believed ought to be available—hearing naught but the unintelligible hum of some universal black hole. Then, very slowly, something incredibly wonderful began to happen. Ever so cautiously, I mentioned my news to people who'd been debating the concept of rational suicide with me for years. Suddenly the critical line was crossed —like the breaking of the sound barrier. Suddenly my world was peopled with persons accepting my intent of suicide, ready to help me end my life at a moment of my choosing, people ready to help make my remaining days vital. My life and my home were transformed into a very real Exit House, staffed first by family and friends whose years with me proved to be years in which we all had trained together, exploring heretofore concealed and forbidden options for commanding our creative lives. Then, to my astonishment, as my personal Exit House became a reality, people outside gradually began to know of it, and, without benefit of training or recruitment, some of them spontaneously volunteered supportive service.

Because I am truly ready to end my life to spare family, friends, and self unnecessary suffering, living is intensified and I'm surrounded by people who have become free to share their sorrows directly with me and each other. Our lives and resources are not consumed with searches for magic cures, although we have explored every current alternative approach to dealing with cancer. Living is heightened because I understand that, had I been able to live into my seventies as I expected, there would have been still larger numbers of people ready to respectfully hear my wish to end my life and ready to help me do so.

But for now, these are remarkably vital months for all of us. My family and friends have enabled me to turn my own home into a real Exit House. It is full of the best relationships of my life, song, laughter, and the promise of ease in slipping peacefully out of my body before it turns to wrecking us all.

II

FROM THE LANDSCAPE OF MY LIFE

Which personal roots are relevant for the clarification of Exit House? Do I call your attention to an anecdote as I see it now or as I saw it at an earlier time? If I point to a fact, will you be able to see it as I now do? Or will it appear to you as it formerly did to me?

The value of these personal revelations is not, I hope, the tragedies or the triumphs I experience, not the neuroses or the stability I reveal. Beneath this autobiographical condensation of sixty-one years is the fact that, from birth onward, a self emerges and ultimately shapes itself. Can a person take what it is born with, see its span, and create its own form? It seems possible to me.

The part of me I like best, and for which I have the most respect, is that small part of me which feels I am my own creation. It is not a pitiful person I want you to see, nor a powerful person, extraordinary and unique. Quite the contrary! I want you to see the incredible life force in a child—a force finding its own way through darkness and crevices.

I was born on a snowy night on February 3, 1917, at my parents' home in Cambridge, Massachusetts. Dr. Mary Parker (a woman doctor in 1917! Now that begins to tell something of my parents!) drew me from my mother's groin and pronounced me "the most perfect baby" she'd ever seen. I was named Mary in her honor. Mary Clodfelter. None other than the eventual ultimate Jo Roman!

It was a truly blissful time for my parents. Their first child, also a girl, had died in infancy. I was a treasured replacement from God. They prayed grateful thanks to Him for their new daughter and promised to mold me to the perfection He wished. They would guard me from sin and raise me to be a loving doer of good deeds in His Holy Name. They showed me to my four-year-old brother, Fred. In a moment of his innocence he perceived my personhood for a fleeting moment and asked, "Do you think *she* would mind if I touched her?"

Father: Reverend Charles Winfield Clodfelter. Mother called him Claude. Aged forty-two. Mother: Adeline Lawrence. Father called her Addie. Aged twenty-seven. How great their love of each other and their devotion to God. Only nine years earlier they had married. She with a rural high school diploma. He not even that. Mother was the only and adored girl child of a large Missouri farm family of American pioneer stock.

Father was the first of his family to leave the Missouri farm. He discovered "reading rooms" in Kansas City, where he read incessantly to ease his torments from repulsive acne. His Bible Belt Fundamentalist world assured him his acne was God's punishment for sins and promised him hellfire and brimstone. In the city he sold various inventions, painted houses, and was inspired by the writings of Emanuel Swedenborg, an eighteenth-century philosopher and mystic who described visions of a God so merciful that He would offer opportunities for redemption even beyond the grave.

Claude's life took direction and hope. His skin cleared to scar tissue. Joy of joys, sweet virginal Adeline with her glorious crown of long, thick, golden-red curls would be his! She would venture with *him* wherever *he* would lead. With missionary zeal mounting, in 1911 they went to save souls in the slums of New York City. They left New York to enter the Swedenborgian Theological School in Cambridge. It was shortly before his ordination that Claude looked upon his beautiful Addie, wet with the sweat of her labor, to see a perfect girl infant between her legs.

A few months later, the four of us moved to the Reverend Clodfelter's first parish, in Fall River, Massachusetts. In 1917, Fall River was a mill town, flourishing on the ill-paid labors of first-generation immigrants, nearly all Catholics. My parents' mission was to persuade them to see the more merciful God discovered by the true genius Swedenborg through his visionary encounters with God's angels. Simultaneously, my parents had other missions. Forming their daughter was one of them.

God told my parents He had given them a perfect girl infant and that if they would nourish and shape her into a God-loving woman doer of good deeds, He would let them enter Heaven to personally look upon Him and become One with Him. He told them this daughter was their personal possession and responsibility until they would turn me over to Him. If He remembered to tell them that I was inside that infant, somehow they didn't hear that. So Addie and Claude doted on their infant daughter, planning my life.

At first I must have felt myself simply a part of the family foursome. There was no trauma, just a nice ongoingness, and then a growing consciousness. When I was about two, Fred started school, making me aware of myself, of my not going to school, of Fred's difference from me, of my parents regarding us differently. For as Fred was moving into his freedom, I was moving into a terrible captivity. By the time I was to start school, the entrapment my parents so lovingly had set for my protection had been conscientiously perfected. It was tightly designed and constructed primarily of one ironclad rule: Under no circumstances was I to talk or play with other children except occasionally under close parental supervision. While Fred could play with whomever he wished before and after school, I was for the next years—until I was eleven, as it turned out—never free to be out of sight of my parents, brother, or a parent-approved adult, such as my teacher.

From the start I longed to end my parents' domination, however well meant. It served to keep me from my real self. My mother's rules became more rigid, the details of my discipline more minute. I was told I must lift my head and look directly into peoples' eyes when talking to them. I whimpered and whispered, "I can't." Mother framed a verse and hung it by my bed: "'ican't' is a little dwarf I know, 'I WILL' is a GIANT STRONG. . . ." And another: "To see a little girl who smiles, I'd travel many many miles. But if I found she cried all day, I'd travel miles the other way." I stole pennies and nickels out of the church offering plate. Shame! Not once was I allowed a penny to spend freely. "Money's not good for you." I lied frequently. Mouth washed out with Fels Naptha yellow soap. There was punishment after punishment, daily spankings. "Don't know what you did wrong today but surely you did something wrong or had bad thoughts about your parents, so here's a spanking for that."

I suffered humiliation and the pain of having to reject invitations from my peers and their parents. I raged at my captors and tried to outsmart them. I whined and pleaded for more freedom. Their answer was always: "In the eyes of God your mother is responsible for you. He, in His Divine Wisdom, guides her to direct you. It may not seem fair to you, but it is God's will."

Father frequently took me on his daily ministerial rounds. I behaved better and was more comfortable with him than with Mother. Arriving at a parishioner's home, Father would direct me to a corner where I was to play quietly. I was to politely refuse food or favors offered me. It was assumed the parishioners couldn't afford to share whatever they offered, or that the food might not be suitable for me. Much of the time I didn't pay attention to the babbling voices. But from time to time the visits would get so theatrical that I'd be very alert. Nothing was more attention-getting than serious illness, dying, death, and funerals. Weddings weren't all that fascinating, but the funerals were something else!

Funerals—at least the many I attended—were not in church. Rather, the dearly departed would be laid out in a casket or sometimes a bed in her or his own home. The shades were always drawn, so the room would be dimly lit. People would gather in another room, moving occasionally to where the body was to stare at or cry over or kiss the corpse. It didn't matter to me which room I was in. They were both very interesting.

In the room where the casket was people wouldn't even know I was there. I could watch how they touched and cried. When no one was doing that, and I was alone, I would stand by the coffin and do my own staring. It would seem like the corpse was breathing, as though it was just asleep. And then the eyes would seem to open. When that happened I would scrunch my own eyes shut tight and in a moment or so I'd look again. Walking home with Father, I asked lots of questions about how one could be sure a person was dead rather than asleep.

Eventually I played a game with corpses, getting to sort of turn off and on the corpses' seeming to be alive. By then, I really knew dead was dead. I could tell by looking or touching. They were cold and hard and lifeless. They felt really different from any live person. A corpse really wasn't a person.

Whenever you walked by a house and saw a spray of flowers on the door, you could tell someone there was dead. There were no flowers at those funerals except on the door. If the ribbon was black or purple, the deceased was adult. If it was white, a child had died. The sprays were so very beautiful.

There was something else about funerals that particularly affected me—actually was more puzzling to me than death itself. Between deaths there was nearly daily talk about Heaven. It was beautiful the way my father described Heaven—with angels and everyone feeling divine. People listened and seemed to really love all that talk, and believe it, too. I really wished Heaven would be real. It sounded much nicer than where I lived. And the Bible pictures were pretty.

I saw it was true what my father said, that most people were surprised to learn from him that even if they were sinners they could get to Heaven. He was always exhorting them to mend their ways. Especially if they drank or played cards. (If there was dancing then, I didn't know about it. But I'd have known it was a sin.) I observed that practically everyone was full of sin and everyone thought it would be great to join God in Heaven. When someone died things got turned around. My father would eulogize how he was sure God had forgiven the beloved's sins and taken him directly into Heaven. If you got in automatically when you died, why all the fuss about sin beforehand? I never once heard a eulogy where Father wasn't assuring everyone that the departed was with God in Heaven. Not even when the late one had been falling down drunk the night before and his wife was still bruised from the last beating. On top of that phenomenon, all those relatives who thought it would be so great to get to Heaven would wail and carry on as though their Lamb of God had just plunged into the eternal damnation of Hell. I really puzzled a lot over those things.

By the time I was ten it was clear to me that a personified God was a figment of the imagination, conjured to explain the otherwise unexplainable and to justify various otherwise unjustifiable rules. The God so clear and absolute to my parents was so different from the equally absolute God of my grandparents. Different still, I gathered, from the parents of those children playing outside my window. Different from the God of my public school teachers. When we said the Lord's Prayer in school— Pearl Friedman, too!—I was instructed to say different words to it so as to make it clear I was not Catholic. I was to say "Forgive us our debts" when "they" said "Forgive us our trespasses." I hung my head in embarrassment at my forced difference.

In 1928, a few people in Lancaster, Pennsylvania, wanted a Swedenborgian pastor to develop a parish, and our little family of five—brother John was aged three now—moved there. Addie and Claude felt refreshed by the new setting. They thought that Lancastrians seemed less foreign, were close to farming and good clean living, and were not predominantly Catholic. They had to build a parish from nearly zero. In doing so they realized it would be valuable to draw young people, especially for Fred, who was fifteen. And it would be safe to give eleven-year-old Mary some leeway. A little.

I rushed through the opening like pent-up water being released. I knew at the outset not to spoil my luck by appearing disobedient. I tried to make my parents happy. They were pleased and relieved with my smiling transformation, so soon there was a new rule. I was able to speak to other children—at last! I could play with them providing we played at my home—where Mother and Father could assess their suitability and the possibility of luring them to Sunday School. I met such restrictions by sharpening my capacity for deviousness. I discovered I could have a double life: one for my parents and the other, squeezed into little crevices, for myself.

Although I was a newcomer, I was welcomed by my peers, perhaps because I was so boundlessly happy to be with them on any terms. They were fascinated to discover how I lived behind my parents' back. Some of their parents resented that I wasn't allowed to be in their homes even though their children could play at mine. Before long, they let me slip secretly into their homes. I knew they wouldn't tell.

Addie started Girl Scouting in Lancaster, and she counted heavily on my friendliness to draw young girls. The girls had fun coming to my house for Scout meetings. Sometimes they were persuaded to attend my Sunday School. But was it my Sunday School? Not exactly. My parents wanted me to teach a class. I went to Sunday School only because I couldn't get out of it. And about teaching I was audacious. Father said it was required of me. "But," I countered, "God would not want me to teach what I don't believe. I can tell children stories which help them understand the importance of being good and kind, but I cannot honestly tell them that I believe in God." An awkwardness for the minister's family, but a reality.

By twelve I had my first close friends. I was a new person and felt I had to make the change official. Real. I wanted to change my name. "I'll be Mary Jo Anne," I said, and my friends were intrigued. Whoever would have thought of such an idea? We all giggled and called each other by our new names. I registered at a new school as Mary Joanne. I *became* Mary Joanne, and I loved this making of myself. I changed several times. Each new name was a new identity, a push toward a new future, a severance from an unwanted past. I graduated from high school as Mary Joan. My parents were confused when they heard me called for my diploma, but they never really questioned me. Later, when I was called Mary Jo, they acquiesced to my desire for a new role and also called me by that name. Eventually the Mary dropped away and I became Jo.

Though my high-school grades were poor, I was accepted conditionally at Millersville State Teacher's College on the outskirts of Lancaster. For the first time, I felt that my true self was emerging. A new name, new surroundings, and a new thirst for growth and knowledge. Among my many new friends was Mary Butts, the first good friend I ever had who believed in God in the intense way my parents did. Somehow, she understood me and helped me and was as sweet and lovely and as good a person as I'd ever known. In college, neither Mary nor I dreamt of how our lives would eventually be entwined. Instead, we spent hours sitting on campus lawns talking and talking. I listened mostly to Mary's dreams of being a minister's wife and doing God's will and having children. As unlike as we were, as disinterested as I was in giving credence to the many concepts of God which surrounded us, Mary listened attentively as I told her of my social life and dreams. She wasn't compelled to criticize or control my thinking and feeling. She had a way of marveling and vicariously enjoying my hard won freedom.

We were college juniors when we confided that each of us seemed to be finding our dreams come true. Mary, who had rarely dated, was in love with Elden Ehrhart, a divinity student at another college in Lancaster. I was falling in love with Bill Wade, who hadn't even finished high school! Mary's love made sense. Mine didn't, and I tried to ward it off.

Bill worked in a wholesale hardware firm with my friend Connie's boyfriend, Jobie—both friends from adolescence who hadn't been able to go on to college. Bill pressed Connie and Jobie to bring us together. I found Bill funny-looking, but finally I reluctantly obliged. It was surprisingly nice being with him, but I never thought it would get serious. At school, I was popular and there was no shortage of dates. Bill pressed for more of my time, and despite my avoidance, I liked him better and better, and finally, I was surprisingly in love with him. The secret, as I learned decades later, was that he, like I, felt himself separated from family and was the maker of himself. But we didn't notice or talk of that. Bill and I talked endlessly, of the lives we wanted to make for ourselves.

We began to shape our dreams into reality. I was a virgin, indoctrinated effectively against premarital sex. We wanted to marry; Bill's mother didn't care. (His father was dead.) My parents liked Bill but wanted us to postpone marriage. We married secretly in March 1937, continuing to live apart. I completed college and went to work as a grade school teacher. Bill worked as an accountant and studied nights at University of Pennsylvania's Wharton Business School. When Bill graduated from Wharton in June 1939, we publicly pleased my parents and privately reconfirmed our devotion with a big church wedding. We established two homes—one for Bill's mother, a new one for ourselves. On June 30, 1940, our son, Tom, was born. On February 21, 1942, our daughter Timmy arrived. We became Middle Americans and held title to our home, a car, and a boat. But we were not about to be traditionalists. Our central excitement was in our dream of being nonpossessive parents who would work together to help our children become themselves. We made a pact. We would love our children and help them discover themselves.

March 27, 1943, was the sixth anniversary of our marriage. Tom was two and a half. Timmy was one. Bill was almost thirty. That morning, Bill was scheduled to have a hernia operation. I was barely twenty-six. My friend Pat arrived at dawn to stay with our sweetly sleeping children while we went to the hospital. I stroked and kissed them, happily noting the color in Timmy's cheeks, framed by her pale yellow silken curls. I laughed softly at the way Tom had pulled his sock over his hand and held it in his own special way against his upper lip. Mother would have objected, but I was very happy.

By late morning, Bill was doped with local anesthesia for the operation, but not so much that he didn't appreciate my being with him. We held hands and talked of the children. We spoke of how quickly this would be over. Thinking I might have liked to be a doctor, I arranged to watch the operation.

Before leaving for the operating room, Bill told the

doctor his arm hurt, so the doctor gave him general anesthesia. No big deal. I watched the surgery and all went
smoothly. We returned to Bill's room for recovery, the
nurse checking the pulse in his right hand, I holding Bill's
left. Suddenly a strange sound rolled out from deep inside
Bill. The nurse ran. Doctors came running and made me
leave. I sat on the stairs outside the room watching the
commotion of oxygen tanks being wheeled into the room.
I remember thinking, "Wait till I tell Bill about this!"
I knew something was seriously wrong, but no one came
to tell me that they had opened Bill's body again, right
there in his room. I could not bring myself to leave my
view of the door, no matter how many times the nurses
tried to direct me to a lounge. I saw a neighboring patient's phone. Even in my numbness I was baffled to find
myself calling my mother at her job, rather than my
nearby and more available father, with whom I felt closer.
Why Mother? Is it a desperate call for magic? A sense of
her having some unique power? She came to the hospital
and sat on the stairway with me. I saw her love and pain,
but did not want to talk or touch. She had no magic to
offer. The doctor approached, crestfallen, and my heart
nearly broke over his pain in having to tell me what I already realized. Bill was dead. He'd had a coronary.

It was several days before I could have people over,
people who wanted to pay their respects and help ease my
agony. I remember entering my kitchen door. Pat was
feeding Timmy in her high chair. I could not look into
Timmy's eyes and for that terrible moment make of her
an orphan. I suddenly could not bear myself. The very
corpse of me sat frozen in the next room. My being was
as dead as Bill's except for some unfathomable anguish.

My eyes kept seeing Tommy try vainly to establish
contact with me. He found the ultimate test of eating each

piece of candy from the bowl on the coffee table at my knees. I saw the look in his eyes as he wondered why I didn't redirect him. I saw all those people coming in. Their solemn looks. Their silence. The future was absolutely blank. It didn't exist.

There was no funeral. Bill and I had agreed that people will feel what they feel. We wanted no performances. No ritualistic corpse-viewing. I wanted to keep my own memories.

At last everyone was persuaded to leave me alone in our home. The children were asleep when the last person left. I walked through the house in the dimness of the night's dark fall. I was dry-eyed, but shriveled inside and stripped of the will to live. I longed to be dead too. My father often told me that someday I would have an experience which would mature me and turn me to God. A moment such as this? It didn't happen. In a moment of wild hope for magic I had called Mother. It never occurred to me to call God. Bill was dead. I wished I were too. I thought it over and over again. "Bill is dead. I wish I were too. And I could be. I could end my life. But . . ."

I stood over the sleeping children. I could take my life only if first I could take theirs, for I could not abandon them that way. And I knew as profoundly as I would ever know anything that their lives did not belong to me. I had neither the wish nor the right to end their lives. I could not die.

Although I was out of my parents' prison into what had been a glorious swooping freedom, I now plunged into what sort of life? At least, I thought, the children are well, and I am free. But oh what a load! How could I bear it? How could I support us? How could I open Bill's closet door? How could I help the children? What did dead mean to them? When Timmy's toy broke and Tommy said, "When Daddy comes home he'll fix it," how could I tell them Daddy would not be coming home? Yet I knew I must survive, and I decided that I would.

On the day of the burial, I sat in the yard and the sun shone on Tommy, Timmy, and me. We began to heal even as I tried to tell them the truth, grateful we did not have our suffering wrenched by ceremonies. From this landscape grow fibers for Exit House, for my survivors as I die.

The obvious road was for me to take a teaching job in Lancaster and try to support the three of us. But I decided I must strike out on my own some other way. I must distance myself from pity. I must find a new way of my own. I searched myself and researched the library. I had long been interested in art and design, and had done some interior decorating in Lancaster. That was something I could do. And I remembered talks Bill and I had had about picking up and moving. We both liked the idea of moving to Alaska. World War II was on, and Alaska was a new frontier, buzzing with the great influx of high-level military and professional people. I realized I could start an interior design business there despite my limitations, because I would have no competition. Before I sold our home and left Lancaster I already knew which Juneau, Alaska, neighborhood we'd move into for its schools.

I doubt that anyone in Bill's family knew or cared that we were leaving Lancaster. But my friends cared and, although bewildered, supported my move. My parents knew there was no point in protesting. I think my dad felt quite all right about my going off. He was concerned and would miss us, but maybe he was even happy that I could do what I felt I wanted to do. I think my mother felt awful and wanted to protest. Now I sort of admire her self-control at the time. Mostly I just marvel and wonder over my own strength in that incredible time.

The journey took five days by train plus five days at sea, and all of us wore brown-and-white-striped seersucker suits to identify us as being together. We traveled knowing we were loved and wished well by all those dear to us. All along the way friendly hands reached out to ease our passage. Our adventure was so absorbing that there was never reason to mourn or look back. We were on our way. It was a year since Bill had died.

What fibers of my Alaska days feed Exit House's roots? Such life changing events took place. So much healing. Such zestful pouring of energy and determination and love and spirit and work and building of new goals and dreams and delight in the children's development. There were marvelous new friends for us all. And the astonishing happenstance of being drawn into the enriching and socially dazzling life of Governor Ernest Gruening and his wife, Dorothy.

Before leaving Lancaster I had written to the chamber of commerce in Juneau, and my letter had been brought to the attention of Dorothy Gruening. I was introduced to her at a tea shortly after our arrival, and she invited me to the Governor's Mansion to meet her husband. Together they introduced me as their guest of honor as they moved me around.

Along the way Ernest made a point of introducing me to his aide, Lieutenant (later Lieutenant Commander) Warren Caro. I really liked his face—handsome and inviting without being threateningly seductive. Warm. He looked so distinguished in his dress uniform with its gold epaulet.

I realized why his face seemed so familiar—on the boat trip from Seattle to Juneau, he had been aboard, and each evening after dinner he had informally played the piano in the lounge. I had studied his face each evening, after the children were tucked into their bunks, as I sat in the lounge dreaming of our new lives.

Now our lives were taking shape—our future was being cast in early 1944.

Yet, these healing colorful events are not the fibers feeding Exit House. Rather, I point to the hours of my nightly insomnia. I could not lay my head on my pillow without it flooding with either design work or, more relevant, relentless wishes to be dead; stark haunting feelings of being inadequate to help the children grow as Bill and I had meant, as I wished. I knew I was giving them the very best I was able to, but I was so distracted by all that needed doing. It was wartime and there was no assistance. I worked as an interior designer and tended the children simultaneously. Exhaustion threatened. I decided my fears were an utterly private matter. No one knew. *I* knew, and the knowledge was painful. I worked into the wee hours and took Seconal to sleep. I keenly felt its eroding effects. The children were up at dawn and were adorable and responsible as they dressed and fed themselves and played in our yard until I got up. But I felt terrible at not being up with them. Sometimes I snapped at them, and I could not bear myself then. I felt that no matter how well everything seemed to be going, I would never have strength enough to make us whole.

My energy drained and I had the underlying wish to die. How could I protect the children from that? I knew I might be hurting them going on like that, but I saw no way to solve my problem. I didn't know of such things as counseling. I began thinking of finding a safer alternative for the children and finally thought of Mary Butts Ehrhart, my wonderful friend from college. She was good and longed for children, and she knew my values, and she wasn't able to have children of her own. The children would be safe with her if they could be together and find a loving closeness.

The children moved into Mary and Elden's lives. I told myself it was temporary, but I was being devious, for I knew that part of me was already thinking that I'd be free to die if the children were lovingly safe apart from me. I cannot speak of my feelings as I waved good-bye to Timmy and Tommy as, accompanied by a friend, they went off as ebulliently as ever on their trip to Mary's. I didn't know to allow myself ventilation of the profound pain.

For a couple of years I maintained my spirited parental role while simultaneously setting out to develop a career which could enable me to support us all. But the children were thriving under Mary and Elden's guidance. They were growing without me, and growing well. It felt good for Tom and Timmy, for their foster parents and for myself, when we arranged for Mary and Elden to become the children's legally adoptive parents in 1946. Good in the sense of loving safety for the children. Good for my friends, who wanted but could not conceive children. And good for me in my sense of safety and relief over the children. Of course, my deep feelings of loss were compounded.

Early in 1946, I went to Pennsylvania to visit Mary, Elden, and Timmy and Tommy, as well as my parents and younger brother. My father was warmly understanding about the adoption proceedings, trusting that whatever conclusion I'd reached had been lovingly weighed. I was sad to see him rapidly aging into his retirement. Mother tried valiantly to contain her bitterness at having no say about the adoption, and at being forced late in life into the job market in order to support herself and Dad. Mother's adored son John, my younger brother, announced he was leaving her to marry. I felt more compassion than affection for Mother, glad for her that my brother decided to remain in the neighborhood.

After my visit to Pennsylvania, I moved to New York, unfamiliar with my life's new configuration. I had returned to New York for two reasons—to start my life over again and to be with Warren Caro, who had moved back following his discharge from the Navy. We were involved in a serious relationship, even considering marriage. My children were safe and I was becoming a nonparent (although I have kept in close contact with Mary and Elden for the rest of my life—and have always seen my children regularly and lovingly). I also was unemployed and near the bottom of my bank account.

I'd been of significant help in supporting and enabling Warren to move into the theater world. He had abandoned his successful law career, which he had entered mainly to please his parents. Now Warren was helping me weigh what sort of options I might find for my childless, spouseless life. It was a discouraging subject because my options were limited by my poor education, lack of money, and vague focus. I knew I didn't want to do the one thing I was paper-qualified to do: be an elementary school teacher. Educationally I'd had barely more than a poor high school training. I'd read very little, and in college never learned how to study. Whatever I did, I'd have to climb up from the bottom. I saw no way to use my art inclinations with economic effectiveness. Outside of Alaska there was no market for my designing talents. I did feel a strong pull to explore what made people and families tick; I was curious about human sexuality. The only way I could involve myself in that direction was to study psychology, but I believed I didn't have either enough ability or funds for that. Warren called a press clipping to my attention. It said a new group had formed in New York City—the American Association of Marriage Counselors.

Without introduction, I called its president, a psychiatrist named Robert Laidlaw, seeking career guidance and direction. He listened to my story and invited me to be his guest at AAMC meetings. Ecstatic, I accepted. There I met leaders in the emerging field—including Alfred Kinsey, whose work would soon revolutionize social consciousness of sexuality. I was invited to go with Robert Laidlaw and his colleagues to the April 1946 National Conference on Family Relations in Philadelphia. There I met and learned of the pioneering work of Dr. Ernest Groves and his wife, Dorothy Groves. They had established the first department of family relations within a university setting, at the University of North Carolina at Chapel Hill. Ernest directed the department within the graduate school of sociology. They were about to host their annual event, the Groves Conference, which attracted an unusually large and wide range of people, both scientists and nonscientists. Dr. Laidlaw arranged for my admission.

It felt as if a door was opening and I was awash in the the fresh air. On the last day of the Groves Conference I stood before the university's prestigious president, Dr. Frank Graham, barely able to believe what he was telling me. He said Dr. Groves wanted me as his graduate assistant and the university was willing to waive its usual academic requirements and give me a scholarship, starting immediately. Perhaps six weeks had passed since I had called Laidlaw.

I felt a rush of vigor and a glorious freedom from the hard soil. I breathed more deeply than I had since Bill's death. Suicidal fear had simply vanished. My insomniac nights were filled with voracious reading—my assistant-ship required me to teach undergraduates, and I worked hard to learn what I had to teach. I began to master the insomnia and could go as long as ten nights without resort-ing to sedation. I grew so strong that I even dared lecture on family issues at neighboring Duke University's law school.

It was all right that the children were growing their way and I mine. It was really all right being unmarried and a nonparent. I felt great as my new person! I'd berated myself for having a weak educational background, but now I saw that my life itself had been educational. I found in myself strengths and resources upon which I could build. I was all right! No, I was better than all right! I was bursting into bloom with self-confidence.

My six-week springtime arrival into this euphoria seems breathtakingly swift, but it compares poorly to the swift-ness of the summer severance of my bloom when, unexpectedly in August of 1946, Groves died and, auto-matically, UNC's department of family relations suffered its demise.

Among my new associates there was no suitable open-ing for me. UNC was obliged, I insisted, to complete my scholarship. Thinking I could find another area in psychology which could advance my interest in the family, I sought and was reluctantly granted a transfer to the university's graduate school of psychology. I discovered it was oriented to experimental rather than clinical psy-chology and didn't realize their extreme difference. Dr. Harry Crane was the department's only clinical psycholo-gist. I was assigned to him as graduate assistant and in-structor.

It was not too difficult for me to quickly learn how to administer and score tests, nor to teach elementary work. But the experimental psychology courses I was required to take were a different matter. I had no background in chemistry, physics, math, or scientific method, making it almost impossible to cope with laboratory courses and the notoriously difficult psychological statistics. As if that weren't enough of a setup for failure, I persuaded authorities to let me take elementary courses in anatomy and physiology at the university's medical school. Perhaps their incredulous indulgence signaled an expectation that I would quickly drop out. They were wrong.

I was assigned to share an office with two men, whom I'll call Sam and Bob. Sam and Bob were very bright graduate scholars and instructors, several years younger than I. Instantly, spontaneously, they felt challenged to get me through, and they proved to be generous, patient, and fun-spirited slave drivers. They never faulted me for not having the background I needed to understand my work. They taught me how to think scientifically. They challenged and criticized my thinking, and worked with me with utmost patience through the stickiest of problems.

I did remarkably well during these twelve months of study, and it is amazing to me that my body withstood the pressures. I suffered heavy bleeding during menstrual periods, and just before my thirtieth birthday had to have a hysterectomy. Earlier I was hospitalized with a rare infection which made my eyes and nasal and sinus passages swell shut and necessitated lancing of both ears. I was a heavy tobacco smoker. Although I worked to end my dependency on Seconal and experienced periods of success, insomnia persisted. Occasionally Warren provided respite—a weekend with him in New York City or Washington, D.C. Once he arranged for a magic and royal

Christmas holiday in Puerto Rico as the guest of its Governor, Jose Pinero. I felt well supported by Warren's and my family's love.

Not surprisingly, Sam, Bob, and I became fast friends. Occasionally we gave ourselves a break for steam-letting frivolity. Chapel Hill is a "dry" town so we would hitch or bus to Durham, a "wet" town, and buy ourselves a bottle. We would tie one on, visiting various student hangouts along the way, and then, several hours later, get ourselves back to our respective rooms. Sam was a minister's son, and somewhat irreverently we taught Bob to harmonize hymns with us. Bob provided us with sophisticated bawdy songs acquired from his undergraduate days at Kenyon.

Bob and I became lovers. I could hardly believe it since I was still involved with Warren. My ears rang guiltily with my mother's words of disgust at the consideration of my ever being sexually involved with anyone other than Bill, who, she believed, was faithfully awaiting my arrival in Heaven. Warren, with the wisdom of his ten-year seniority and his less guilt-ridden sexuality (combined with our geographic distance), proved quite capable of accepting my affair at Chapel Hill, and I was glad not to feel pressed to deceive.

Exam time approached. Academic matters were under reasonable control but were getting more hectic. I could cope, if only I could get a good night's sleep. Nearly out of Seconal and without a local doctor, I stopped on Main Street at the one doctor's office I'd noticed. A woman in a nurse's uniform was at a desk in the filled waiting room. I asked when I might see the doctor. She told me she could not say unless I first told her why I wanted to see him. I softly told her I was tense with exam pressure and would like some Seconal. She sprang to an angry stance, saying sharply, "My husband does not supply addicts!" All heads swiveled to stare at me. I fled.

Addict! I'd never thought of myself as an addict. I thought they were dope fiends who lived in big-city ghettos. Criminals. I'm no addict! I thought. I don't use Seconal because I like it! I need it! I experienced my very first taste of panic. No Seconal equaled a threat to the last critical hours of pre-exam study. What to do? Still not accepting the addict label, I went to the university infirmary. My panic showed and, sensibly, I was steered to the university's psychiatrist, the wife of none other than the university's clinical psychologist. I was lucky. The woman was a mature professional who skillfully enabled me to discuss my wearing battle with suicidal thoughts and insomnia. She supported and encouraged my effort and appreciated the struggle. She told me of relaxation exercises and prescribed Seconal.

Several days later, I set a pitcher of water and a glass on my bureau beside my new supply of Seconal. The cache was lethal in size. I reached a decision—to end my life. True, it was a life very worth living and full of promise. But, true too, I was simply exhausted! I knew of no sleep long or deep enough to restore my energy so that again it would match my zest for living. I was nearly without money and found intolerable the thought of scrounging for Seconal. I just wanted to be done with suicidal thoughts and fatigue and the relentless uphill climb. I'd had enough.

The relief I felt was energizing. I discarded possessions which were of no interest to others or might be interpreted by them as distressing. I wrote thoughtful notes and prepared them for Bob to mail when I was dead. There was sadness in making my good-byes and trying to shape them so the recipients would have the best opportunity possible to take our separation in stride. Calmly I took a walk across the campus. How different it all looked and felt. I hadn't really noticed that tree's beautiful form before.

I lingered when meeting fellow students and faculty, mindful of this being our last meeting. The difference in knowing and not knowing my secret made some comments amusing. But mostly I felt special warmth for everyone and told them of the good feelings I had for them.

I sat alone under another tree, reflecting. I did not feel depression or desperation or panic. And yet there were well-meaning people who would wreck my life with incarceration and crippling labels if they knew what I was about to do. I was thinking of the spectrum of people to whom my death meant adjustment rather than just passing, wincing moments. At one end there were the two people, utterly different from each other, who, for equally different reasons, would have the hardest time accepting my death: Mother and Warren.

Warren would probably torment himself with feelings that I would not have become overexhausted and ended my life had he been more ready for marriage. Marriage to Warren would have been healing, but I did not want him to fault himself for not solving my life problem at this time in our lives. I didn't fault him. And I only hoped my note to Warren would head him into eventual realization that neither my life nor my death was his responsibility. Warren had done inordinate good in my life, elevating me to a new planet and opening my mind to new worlds. I did love him. Whatever his foibles, they paled to nothingness beside the pleasures and freedom to grow he had given me. Images of Warren's anguish come closer than any other to staying my hand.

As for my mother, in my mind's eye I watched her agony, wanting to reach out to comfort her and feeling the cold absence of love between us—the sort of love which is so trusting that each may confide and touch the other and share tears as well as laughter. I hadn't begun to understand her willingness to let me be myself and so unhappily still harbored distrust of her. I saw her as unforgiving of me for not letting her make me into the child of her dreams. Why, I wondered, was she inclined to turn failures and disappointments into bitterness? I hadn't yet begun to comprehend how harshly she had experienced life. My compassion for her was in its infancy.

The self-confrontation in my suicide preparations was profound and forever. It was beyond the reach of Bob's earnest loving search for grounds for reversal. My suicide would confront Bob with an awful loss, and I cried in the night at that prospect. But I knew without question that Bob would in no way be crippled. He was young and strong and growing. We both knew the problem was mine, not his. Faced with taking the responsibility for my own death, I was able to face responsibility for the life I had led.

Father? I imagined my father weeping, and I wept with him. I appreciated his respect for me. Father would not berate himself for my death, nor fault me. He would try to comfort Mother, but I knew there was not enough trust between them for healing relief.

My children? In their daily throes of growing up it would be easy enough for me to fade into the background. But I feared the inescapable. Little Tommy and Timmy would eventually have to come to grips with my death. Probably in their adolescence or young adulthood. I could only hope that by then their own resources and their identification with Mary and Elden would be cushioning. The alternative for the Ehrharts of my clinging to life and perhaps failing later did not draw me. Wishfully, and with grounds for trust, I decided I had to take the risk.

I sat on the floor in my room, sorting treasures, sur-

rounded by those things which mattered most to me.
Photographs of my family and of Alaska. Sketches I'd made
and liked well enough to leave in the open. Alaskan arti-
facts. Rugs coloring bed, floor, and walls. Basketry, ivory
pieces. Memorabilia. Albums. Treasure sorting at life's
end can be one of life's high experiences—however confronting. Those treasures seen in the extraordinary light
of the time were aswirl with memories given full sway
because of time's finality. Some sparkled with laughter
and some were wet with tears. What was to become of
them? What would they possibly mean to others? I saw
a measure of my young worn life.

On a Thursday evening, Bob and I had a sentimental
parting. I told him of my appreciation of his love and of
being able to trust him not to blow the whistle. He was
braced by his own resources and all I could add to them.
Our emotions were distinctly flattened by the need each
of us had for self-control. It was easier for me than for
Bob. Bob was walking away flooded with racing turbulent
reflections, relief included among them, for—not meaning
it—he had recently resorted (as a challenge to my position) to suggesting consideration of our having a suicide
pact. Not wanting Bob's death, I had played the fantasy
game out nevertheless, calling his bluff. When he had
withdrawn his fake offer, I had been as relieved as he.
Participation in that fleeting macabre game stands on my
life's landscape not so much as a low point as it does the
height of my life's shame. Even now it pains to look into
those moments and see the dangerous risk and capacity in
myself to be so callously insensitive to the distress behind
Bob's melodramatic ploy. Our views of what was evolving
had to differ. Whatever our views, Bob was going to
escape from his into sleep that evening.

I stood before my mirror that twilight and palmed
several bright red capsules. I'd never tried to swallow

more than one at a time. I filled a glass with water. If I tried to take all those capsules one at a time, I thought, maybe I'd fall asleep before I could take a lethal dose. I wanted to take them all. To make certain. I decided I'd better try to swallow as many as possible each time.

The first group went down well enough. I tried to take more the next time. It was more difficult, and I had to gulp water. I got them all down. I thought how good it was to know my struggle was over. I glanced once more into the mirror and said good-bye to myself—surprised, somehow, at how simple and untormented, how gentle was the end of my life. I took the two steps to my cot and lay down. I smiled at myself for wanting to arrange myself attractively. It occurred to me that I wanted to die with a smile on my face. For a very few moments my mind filled with images of those closest to me. I cannot know the shape my smile took.

Bob's notes of a short while later say:

Confused and preoccupied, I delivered my Friday lecture and attended another class. Then I started to walk, a crude kind of escape and ineffective. A chaotic battle began to rage in my consciousness— revulsion, love, fear, pain—the unsheathed pain of losing a beloved object, self-condemnation. Time crept by. I squeezed out each minute. I walked and kept walking although the effort was exhausting and my body was wooden. I lay down in the pine woods and tried to sleep, but that effort was exhausting. The uncontrolled free-for-all of images and thought segments continued to molest me, never ceasing. As it grew dark I went home and collapsed. . . . Eventually . . . an irrational hope welled. . . . It was a relief to succumb to it. . . . I dressed and went to her room. Her door was locked . . . I banged on it again and again. I heard a noise, and then a drugged voice asked who it was. I lost consciousness for a moment but revived and waited and waited while she crawled and staggered to the door and fumbled with the lock. I carried her back to her bed and she fell back into sleep again almost immediately and did not wake sufficiently to be articulate until several hours later. The aftereffects were nearly as unpleasant as the experience of losing her. For nearly a day she woke and slept intermittently, but when she was awake she was aware only of gross bodily needs and the fact of her failure. The so-called higher patterns of behavior were not yet operating. She demanded food and water, which she downed gracelessly and then lost in wretched nausea. I nursed her and talked to her all night and all the next day. By evening she had slept off the drug sufficiently to stand on her feet and to feel sympathy and compassion. We dressed in our best and went out to dinner and met our friends. No one suspected what had happened.

I had not taken a large enough dose to fulfill my suicide intent, apparently.

My rebirth was, alas, marred with the ugliness of nausea. Too much water? Too fast? No matter, for something truly marvelous had transpired. Slowly I wakened, deeply rested and profoundly changed. I was unaccountably renewed. My overpowering sense of exhaustion was gone. I would never again, as long as I live, experience the wish to be dead!

Now I am planning another suicide—hopefully protected against body rejection—but paradoxically I have never again been suicidal. There is such a distinction to be made!

In the days following my suicide attempt I passed my

exams. My rest made that effort much easier. I was tempted to ask for renewal of my scholarship, gleefully believing I'd earned the right to it. But I knew I'd run enough rats. Whatever my future career was to be, further study of experimental psych wasn't the preparation I needed. I decided to leave Chapel Hill. Bob and I both knew well and accepted—with a little clinging—that the time had come to draw our romance to a close. An outsider might understandably have looked askance at us. However, we had such respect for each other's individuality and appreciation of what we had meant to each other that neither of us expected the other to alter our relationship by forcing it into something it wasn't. Friends forever.

Late spring of 1947 I returned to New York City, hoping to find my way there through my recently gained contacts and friends in the field. Abraham Stone, M.D., and Lena Levine, M.D., directors of the Margaret Sanger Research Bureau, headquarters of birth control and family planning pioneering, made a place for me. I designed and carried out research on how clients acquired their personal information about sex and how they would rather have learned. Most learned clumsily and would have preferred parental guidance. Most also wished they would be able to inform their children but believed they would not be able to do so.

Warren and I enjoyed our reunion. After he knew of my suicide attempt and had seen me through my hysterectomy, we decided to stop talking of our marriage potential and get on with it. Our marriage, November 2, 1947, marked the beginning of my life's next phase. It was very different, indeed, from all that had preceded. Its coloration of Exit House lies in its support of my orthodox psychoanalysis with Henry A. Bunker, M.D. Dr. Bunker's death in 1953 occurred at the two-and-a-half-year mark of my analysis, inadvertently contributing to my increasing awareness of life's tenuousness. I worked my way through another two and a half years with Maria Hoefer, M.D.

Our marriage made another significant contribution to Exit House by supporting the continuation of my education. I earned a master's degree in psychiatric social work qualifying me to work within my range of competence and interest. These developments all occurred quietly and beneath the surface with great good humor and, yes, more love. I now saw my life as charmed, although it continued to prove less than flawless. I found myself truly loving Warren and indebted to him. Alas, however, I also soon found no possibility of being the person Warren needed me to be in his highly theatrical life and simultaneously the kind of person I wanted to become for myself. I knew Warren and I must separate. I found myself unable to continue my own emergence. In 1952, after five years of marriage, we divorced.

Our divorce was wrenching. We were civil and respectful of each other—even loving, I'd say. In due time we recovered and survived and established a platonic friendship to last through our lives.

For me, initiating our divorce took more courage than my suicide attempt. I made the transition from the aftermath of separation from Warren into the venture of being independently on my own. By my own choice! Such a frightening heady venture even at the mature age of thirty-five. It was like choosing to be born. Laborious! I can't help but wish I had been able to mature longer than two years into this phase before meeting Mel Roman. But fate didn't consult me.

Can I, here in 1979, possibly look at my twenty-two years with Mel and read his relevance to my creation of Exit House? Can I do that while, simultaneously, I am en-

gaged in the awesome task of making a gentle leave-taking
of him; of launching him into a new life? Can I? I suspect
the leave-taking will be more readily achieved than such
a reading. How to try?

By the time Mel and I met in 1952 I had worked three
years in the psychiatric setting of Hillside Hospital in New
York and had just moved on into the psychiatric treatment
clinic of New York City's Domestic Relations Court, where
I worked with delinquents and their families. Mel was
emerging in the court as a gifted psychologist. I shared
everyone's pleasure in his gentle strength and his capacity
to turn foibles into endearing qualities. Our work brought
us together more and more.

Our backgrounds were vastly different, and it was fun
exploring them. Mel loved talking about his family of mid-
dle-European Jewish background. It was surprisingly as
different from Warren's German-Jewish background as
from my so-called WASP roots. To enrich my education he
took me to his parents' home for their ethnic food and
storytelling. In contrast to my parents' home life, or Bill's
or Warren's (I never knew Bob's), Mel's parents' home
life was remarkably warm with affection, laughter, and
endlessly repeated anecdotes. They made me feel welcome even though I was a gentile.

Mel's own home seemed equally welcoming to me, but
it was a chilly place, his warmth oddly absent. He and his
wife seemed distant from each other; unrelated except in
conflicting ways around their three-year-old daughter,
Lisa. I was puzzled, and it wasn't until months later
that I understood their separation. Oddly, their problems
stemmed as much from cross-cultural differences between
two Jewish subgroups as it did from more ordinary marital
conflicts. Oddly? Don't Protestants find abrasions when
crossing their subdivisions?

When Mel told me he was headed for divorce, I was not surprised. Nor was it surprising to find us falling in love. I did feel strangely embarrassed over letting myself fall in love with someone a decade younger than I was. Perhaps I was feeling restored to the youth I had lost when Bill died. Perhaps I thought our relationship would be an affair such as I had enjoyed with Bob. But nothing ever came close to disengaging us—until nearly twenty years later, when Exit House took a particular shift in its development.

I left the court to become administrative head and chief psychiatric social worker at University Settlement House's psychiatric clinic. I was finally established as an independent career woman! Mel joined the clinic on a part-time basis. Our affair evolved along with Mel's difficult divorce, although it was not the cause. Mel had few conflicts about leaving his wife, but it was intolerable having his child taken from him. Partly due to that torment, he suffered a coronary. As sobering as that event was, it also served to negate our age difference. Ambivalence about marriage became suddenly insignificant. His divorce came through, freeing us to marry and begin our new lives. From the outset and throughout, our marriage has nourished the best in each of us, making our creativity blossom.

We reorganized our careers, achieving an arrangement which freed Mel from his previous pattern of holding several jobs at once in addition to his private practice. His primary job was at Einstein College of Medicine, where he pioneered, with others, the development of a social and community psychiatry program. It was agreed that he would work less, building in more rest than he'd otherwise have. We established an apartment and an office a block apart from each other so that time and energy were not expended on traveling. I left my job and moved my own small private practice of psychotherapy to our new office. The flexibility in my work hours gave me time to tend development of our quarters and domestic needs. Mel's strength returned steadily; his income moved steadily upward despite his shorter working schedule. If either of us noted that I was earning less and less, we made no issue of the fact.

Through these changes, we made one of the most exciting discoveries of our lives: We were not only interested in art, we were *artists!* We ventured to create what we referred to as interaction paintings, and were invited to exhibit them. Interaction paintings were paintings we worked on jointly, the two of us working on one canvas, which we thought analogous to the way jazz musicians worked. Later exhibits were of our individual works. Soon we rented a loft for our artwork. We began summering in Provincetown, on Cape Cod. They were marvelously refreshing and challenging summers, full blown with painting and sculpting. One summer, 1963, was so rife with civil rights conflicts that we worked in Mississippi for the Medical Committee on Human Rights. This and other experiences with the peace movement proved to be a primary coloration of Mel's artwork for years to come, as well as influencing his bold collaboration to bring innovative mental health services into the city's South Bronx, one of the country's worst ghettos.

Summers in Provincetown became the very source of our energies. At first we lived and worked in Karl Knaths's studio, treasuring our exposure to Karl's mind and his art, challenging each other's thinking. Eventually we could afford to move to the water's edge, and for our last decade we lived in a beach house known as the Standish. Each place we ever lived in we made into a place we loved, but the Standish required practically no effort from us. There was enough work space for each of us. Best of all, it had a spacious living/dining room with a great fireplace. The room opened directly onto our private beach at the edge of Provincetown Bay. Nothing impersonal in life ever served my well-being so profoundly. The constantly and dramatically changing tides and shifts of light and weather flowed through my being, healing and nourishing and tuning me into life's universal eternal force. The flotsam and jetsam, the blue-eyed scallops, the Herman crabs (as little Lisa, Mel's daughter, used to call the hermits), and the Segals (as she called the gulls) came and went.

Our summer friends were such a respite from our socially starved city life. The social circle formed most afternoons on our beach, drifting apart reluctantly with the cool breeze following sunset, reassembling later in the evening at one home or another.

During those years I had been timidly testing reactions to the idea of rational suicide. How much resistance there was to serious discussion of the subject! Friends came to twit me for probing it. Finally, driving to Provincetown one summer's beginning, rapping as usual, I told Mel that I'd come to an idea of how I could articulate what I'd been thinking about rational suicide. I would write about a place called Exit House where people's right to end their lives would be respected and suicide would be responsibly assisted. I would stop bothering myself with questions about how such a place could come to be. Rather, I would simply invent the place and present it as a model to reveal suicide's positive potential. Mel said it was a terrific idea. That was the summer I began spending more time at the typewriter than in the studio. If only I could paint Exit House! Working with words felt like an impossible demand to make of myself. Still, the idea pressed me to the effort.

It pressed also through years of our city living. It was

always simmering in my mind through our incredibly full years, regardless of what I was doing.

I moved from painting into exploring the use of tactility as a medium for art. I developed "touch boxes," whose interiors cannot be seen but can be explored by hand. I was intrigued by many facets of these experiments, particularly by discovering that vertical space seems to feel tactilely different from horizontal space. Simultaneously, I was looking for a building where Mel and I might combine our office, living, and art studio needs. Mel and I had essentially no savings, thanks both to my small earnings and to a post-coronary decision that we would live to the hilt each day without economic concern for the morrow. Still, I couldn't resist the temptation to ask our friends, Rachel and Jackie Robinson, if they would be interested in sharing a pair of brownstones with us. I would take responsibility for altering the buildings' interiors, splitting them horizontally and adding an elevator so Mel could be assured access to the top-floor studio light even if he became ill again. The Robinsons could have the lower floors so they could garden. Their response was a quick yes.

I discovered Manhattan's unusual West Side urban renewal project, where, at the outset, the city was willing nearly to pay people to move in to renovate the borough's notorious slum. I was just about to have a Madison Avenue exhibition of my Touch Boxes—the peak of my art career—at the Castellane Gallery. Suddenly I was plunged into leading the organizing of thirty families to purchase a group of nine contiguous brownstones, referred to as "9g" in my house-search notes. 9G Cooperative, Inc., was thus born. Four years later, still president of the Cooperative, I stepped across our new threshhold with Mel. Rachel and Jackie were next door to us.

Mel and I occupied quarters spread across the top of

three of the nine brownstones. True, we could set the whole place inside our old loft and have space left over. But nary an inch was wasted. We had all we needed, all at one location (except for Mel's Einstein office), and with good subway access. Mel had little energy for all the moving from our old places, but soon felt nearly as excited as I was thrilled by our new home.

We predicted as we moved into 9G that we were verging on more settled lives. I resumed private practice. Resumption of our painting and sculpting was at hand. But once more life proved unpredictable. Two events significantly altered our course.

An exhibition at the Corcoran Gallery in Washington, D.C., of the architectural visions of Paolo Soleri drew us into significant involvement with his effort to create humane ecologically sound cities—arcologies. Eventually Mel became Paolo's close friend and adviser. I produced a plan for development of two restaurants at Arcosanti, the Arizona arcology being constructed. But despite my constant interest, I had little to offer other than encouragement. Mel's work with Paolo greatly restricted his studio time.

The second event was felt more heavily and intertwines with Exit House. It was our involvement in the life and art of an artist named Jochen Seidel. Seidel lived and worked in a loft adjacent to ours. We admired his art and were privy to the trials and tribulation of his personal life. Coinciding with our building and moving into 9G, Seidel concluded that he had completed his statement as an artist. He had no family responsibilities. He was totally uninterested in developing a new career. He wished to end his life. He made several very earnest attempts which were thwarted. He had tried taking pills and gas but each time was found and hospitalized, and each time he recovered.

It was the thwarting of Seidel's suicide that lingered in

the compartment of my mind where Exit House was emerging. Twice I had intervened in his suicide attempts, once convincing him to go into psychiatric treatment.

But Jochen Seidel finally succeeded in ending his life at age forty-seven in 1971. I walked into his loft to find my friend's body hanging from one of the loft's rafters. I felt deep relief that my friend's suffering was ended. I recalled his telling me about wanting to die peacefully and not wanting to hurt himself. I felt anger at the doctors who dared feel proud of having forced life upon a person who didn't want it. I was angry at the doctors who said they had no right to end the life of a person who wanted to die, declaring that that would be playing God. I was angry that those doctors forced my friend to hurt himself as the only means of ending his life. I wanted to cut down my friend's body and take it to a crematorium and recycle its ashes. But no, it was not permitted. The body was not my friend, only a part of his remains.

During the following month of settling into 9G, trying to resume private practice, rescuing Seidel's art collection, and tending our complex lives, the barb of the thwarting of Seidel's suicide persisted in annoying. I managed to ignore it, until . . .

Suddenly Zelee Isum, the mother of my friend Rachel Robinson, collapsed. Without hesitation I started mouth-to-mouth resuscitation. At first my mind raced, trying to recall instructions I'd read. My own heart leaped with excitement as her collapsed chest filled and moved rhythmically with my inhalations. I settled into a rhythm, and now my mind reflected. Suddenly. What was I doing! Why was I (of all people!) trying to revive Zelee, an elderly woman, a semi-invalid, surviving uncomfortably with a pacemaker? Was it not an appropriate time for her to die? Why was I thwarting her dying?

I wanted to stop. No one was in the room to see my withdrawal, but I hesitated. Suppose Zelee had begun to revive with my effort? If I stopped now, would I be killing her? Was it playing God to stop? Or to go on giving her my breath? Who was to judge? Where did the responsibility lie? With whom? My aloneness was acute. I had to decide. What were my alternatives? Naught but to use my best judgment. And what was that?

Tearily, I imagined the main characters. I saw Rachel fighting desperately for Zelee's survival. Rachel's wounds still bled from her husband's and son's deaths, a few years before. If I could, would I save Zelee for her? I'd want very much to do that for her. But it was Zelee's life. Zelee, whom I barely knew. Zelee, whose life appeared to me to have become pained. Collapsed, Zelee was at peace. But in spite of my beliefs, I tried everything to save her. It was too late, however. Zelee died despite my efforts.

It dawned upon me that my anger toward the doctors was somewhat misplaced. Not only had I tried to save Zelee, to thwart her release from a life of questionable quality, but I realized that I—me, myself, I!—had contributed significantly to the thwarting of Seidel's suicide. I was flooded with questions. Could that mean that within me there was some instinct for life preservation at all costs? An instinct more powerful than intellect? Spontaneously I had moved to save Zelee's life although I knew its quality was questionable. Spontaneously I moved to save Seidel's life although I knew and respected his wish to end it.

This challenging personal confrontation led me through a tough convoluted obstacle course to an unanticipated conclusion. Not surprisingly, my search brought me to the deeper conviction that, concomitant with the evolution of life extension, there must emerge a socially supported and protected human right for adults to reject having life forced against one's will. What took me by surprise was the insight that the ideal way for a person to be protected against enforced life is to take responsible command of one's own life span—not only its length. This meant that to be as responsible as possible, I must take command of the end of my own life!

I was not even slightly suicidal in any pathological sense. I was, in fact, zestfully engaged in life. But I saw suicide as a rational, responsible act for me to plan. Fortunately, I was only fifty-eight, and so I believed I had ahead of me many good years which I could count on in which to do the things I dearly wished to do. I wanted those years so I could complete building on my own life span the best person I was able to create, so I could know the fruits of my effort, so I could know more of life.

Through the several years of thinking about issues of Exit House I generally was a lone explorer, although gradually I found other human beings willing to help me with some of the trail cutting. But when I discovered I was to plan my own life's ending, I felt as if I'd launched myself into outer space, where there was no human communication. It was odd and extraordinary how an ordinary human being could go about daily feet-on-the-ground-living with spouse, family, and friends and simultaneously be exploring the outer space of the inner mind.

I found the main issues I had to examine were (1) the consequences of my suicide to my survivors, (2) preparations I wanted or needed to make within myself, (3) preparations I wanted or needed to make with others, (4) selection of time of exit, (5) determination and acquisition of means of exit, (6) provision of assistance. Considerations were so interrelated that sometimes focus was evasive. My life was so full of living which was unrelated to these considerations that I realized I'd be lucky if I found my way through the thicket in good time. I wished I had started years ago. I wished I had company. I wanted company so much that I thought about telling Mel of my decision and ongoing search. I knew how helpful it would be to have his thinking to interact with my own.

Suppose Mel was upset by my telling him I planned to end my life in my later years? The question stopped me in my tracks. I thought about turning back, but could not. There is no exploration without risk, and here I was in a most frightening place.

I arrived relatively easily at knowing that I wanted by age seventy to have sure means of exit and to have developed alertness to watch for a suitable time of exit. I imagined that exit time was not at all likely at seventy but probably around age seventy-five. Perhaps—with unanticipated luck—I'd want to live to eighty. I thought I most certainly would not want to live longer. My time frame was based on some combination of our times with my family's history of long, physically healthy lives. Also, on my observations of their declining years. And, of course, upon my strong sense of personal preferences. So I thought I'd be ready to end my life by age seventy in 1987, and probably would end my life at age seventy-five in 1992. Relatively easy calculations.

But what would that mean to Mel? Suppose for some reason I would want out at seventy. Mel would be only sixty. And sixty could be such an awful age to become a widower! Our age difference struck the only age-related sharp blow I'd ever experienced in our marriage.

The more I thought about it, the more I realized I had to bring myself to talk with Mel of my suicide intent. His life as well as mine was central to the impact. I didn't want to be guilty either of imposing on him or of depriving him of participation in decision-making on such life-central issues. I realized I carried a bomb. Perhaps nothing made me realize the power and wisdom of seeing suicide as a responsible means of completing one's life span than realizing that Mel might not be able to tolerate the intensity of the awareness nor its consequences. The most treasured relationship of my life was at stake. It was ironic that that relationship had nourished my fortitude to the extent that I'd risk having to go on alone. I trembled. It was 1975, and Mel was forty-eight. Long loved by me. Our years together had brought out the best in him. I shared pride in his strength and humanity, his boldness and sophistication. He was inspiring and challenging. I didn't always think of him as handsome, but I did then. He shared all this with me and additionally nourished me with affection and respect. I could not want to hurt him. I knew he was strong. And he was human and shakable. I didn't even want to rock his boat, but that would mean having to dishonor my own beliefs and my trust in his strength.

At forty-eight, Mel was coming into a high time of professional competence and recognition. It was both a good time and a bad time to tell him. It was the only time to tell him. I did.

Looking at the landscape of our relationship across the next three years, 1975–78, the time just preceding cancer's strike, our lives seem to have little bearing on Exit House except at an ever-present underlying level where the very essence of our relationship was tuned to Mel's coping with the impact on him of my plan to exit when he would be in his sixties. The saga of these years seems more his than mine, although, of course, highly interactive.

Mel moved with beautiful strength and momentum. He was loved by many, and most especially by me. Our love was like an elegant mature wine. We quietly savored it and sensed its fragility. Mel's art and profession were sturdy and inspiring to others, but the strain dulled the twinkle in his eyes, and he had new facial lines. His shoulders were stooping as he bent to guard his footing instead of looking forward with head held high, as he had done when the road ahead seemed so clear. He felt the ground slipping from beneath him.

It was my telling Mel I would die around 1992 that triggered the slippage. Why did I insist on looking at that, Mel pressed me. Okay, Jo, die then if you must. And, yes, I think it'd be reasonable of you to end your life then. But why must that be seen by me now? Why? I feel you're abandoning me. I hear you say you won't leave me before it would be timely to do so, and I know without your telling me that it would not be out of the ordinary for you to die a normal death by then. But *knowing* that you will die then is something I hate looking at. It fills me with feelings of abandonment and rage and distracts me from the living I was enjoying.

Was I wrong in telling Mel? I felt no wavering of conviction as far as my own life was concerned. If anything, I felt confirmation of the value of facing death forthrightly. One's own in particular. Those of people with whom one is deeply involved, perhaps equally so. But I saw from Mel's internal rumblings that he felt it would be better to walk on into the future without pausing to look at the inevitable realities of his own death and the death of those close to him. I realized it was I, rather than Mel, who was out of step. But I felt like the one who discovered the earth to be round rather than flat.

At the time I told Mel of my aim to command my life

span's end, Mel's mother had cancer. I tended her through hospitalizations. I had wanted very much not to conceal her cancer from her. However, the family forcefully and unanimously outvoted me. In 1975 she was in remission and appeared to be almost her normal physical self. I knew she had been shut off from open relationships with her beloved family. I believed her being frankly informed of her condition would be less debilitating than that. Mel's mother believed she had cancer but was led by doctors and family to believe she was imagining it. The family, egged on by doctors and social custom and their own compatible beliefs, disagreed with me. Firmly. Well-meaning, too, which I appreciated.

Mel and I sat for hours in the hospital corridor outside his mother's door. I tried to listen and speak with Mel through the voicelessness of our handholding. We had found her unconscious and Mel instantly did as he was programmed to do—exactly as I did with Jochen Seidel and Zelee Isum—and, consequently, relinquished his/our command of forces bearing upon someone so dear to us. We unleashed forces which had no capability of knowing the compassion and knowledge only we had the potential of using. I understood what Mel had done and knew I, myself, might have done the very same. Still, it felt terribly wrong. I wished I would not have called the police, as Mel did. But could I have withstood the frightened demanding censure of a witness, Mom's elder sister? I didn't know then. I don't really know now.

Mom's cancer-ridden body, face lined with the burdensomeness of her long and worn life, lay crumpled on the bathroom floor while an emergency crew tried to jolt her heart into action. As Mel and I sat in the hospital corridor, Mel's distance from me insurmountable, except for the touch and vibrations between us, I thought he was frozen with numbness inside some infinite hollow. From time to time a doctor unknown to us made a very brief appearance. He, too, was essentially voiceless. He needed only to move his bent head from one side to the other to convey that Mom's heart was still beating without improvement in her vital signs. I found nearly unbearable the thought of Mom being brought back to her dreary cancerous life—now probably more pathetic than ever. Why, I wanted to shout, are we letting this monstrous thing happen? Good heavens, have we no conscience! No mercy! I wanted to dart into the room and unplug Mom. I argued with myself about rights. Who has the right to do that? Well, who has the right *not* to do it?

I told myself I had no right. She was Mel's mother, not mine. Anger flushed. That was not enough reason. I thought: She may be his mother and he may love her very much and very differently than I, but that can't negate the fact that Mom and I have shared genuine loving closeness and I do love her enough to hate what is being done to her and I want to stop it. She was a human being and I wanted to scream at my cowardice for not acting on my convictions. I wanted to urge Mel to stop this terrible scene. But I was held at bay by my fear of imprisonment, love of Mel, my awareness of his struggle, and my willingness to sacrifice Mom for him. So I sat in the enveloping silence. Waiting, patient. Patient and numb.

A flurry of family arrived and leaned against the wall. Now I imagined all hope of intervention was gone, for they seemed programmed to reinforce Mel's programmed self. Mel seemed to welcome their reinforcement. He seemed relieved to let go of my hand. There was talk, and the doctor said there was no point lingering, as Mom's condition could go on for a very long time. Relatives left to inform the family assembling at Mom's home. Mel and

I lingered a little longer. Mel walked away, then returned to tell me he asked the doctor to let her go. I felt more than ever his love of Mom and of himself. It was good sharing that love.

Mom died the first day of 1976. The entire family mourned her loss, each in a private way. Surely Mel's mourning was unique because of our own confrontation of the time.

But now Mel's loss of his mother was coupled with his feelings of being abandoned by me. He felt increasingly put upon at any raising of related issues. The struggle was locked inside him. For the most part I could only stand by, trying to reassure him that I was not at all inclined to abandon him; that I wanted us to continue on together; and that I regarded it as unjustifiable for us to go forward pretending we had no major separation to be incorporated into our lives. I wanted both of us to see that the life span of all relationships must come to an end and that we could benefit by helping each other prepare for our inevitable separation.

When Bill, my first husband, died, I felt over and over again that the shock was unnecessarily intense and crippling. In subsequent years I came to understand those feelings were entirely accurate. The shock of losing the reality of Bill would have been quite enough. But shock's impact had, indeed, been unnecessarily exacerbated by two factors in particular. One, my youthful and partially neurotic overidentification with Bill. Two, and more relevant, intensification of my shock came from our social structure. The latter renders it nearly impossible for any of us to replace wishes and illusions of immortality with acceptance of the reality of our earthly mortality. It is the unrealistic and crippling nature of this social structure that I challenge.

It matters not what one's religious or philosophical beliefs are. Nor whether one would end her/his own life or not. Nor whether one believes in one's personal being having had a previous existence and/or an existence to come beyond the demise of the earthly body. The reality is that one's earthly body is mortal. Further, its resident must be disadvantaged as long as that reality is not faced. One may embalm a body, freeze it, plug it into diminishing energy channels, combine it with parts of other bodies. One may see it buried and believe its person is also being buried. One may believe whatever one chooses. But humanity is always served best, I believe, when one learns to distinguish between reality and unreality.

Your body will die. So, too, the bodies of each of us—including those closest to us. Believe what you want about what, then, becomes of your personhood. But let us at least accept and prepare ourselves forthrightly for the recycling of our bodies.

My development following Bill's death brought me through relevant changes. For a while it seemed too risky to allow myself full closeness to another person, as though closeness would place me in a position where I might once more be jolted by death of a loved one. Coming to grips with that fearsome possibility helped me sort out issues, to feel safe to relate closely to others, and because I had done major sorting of issues, I could be truly close and yet never again in danger of devastation of my personhood. There has been no time in my involvement with Mel when I would not have been rocked if he had died. But never again would I use or let others use anyone's death destructively against myself.

How vividly I recall the struggle within me when Mel lay critically ill with a coronary.* How informative it is,

---

* By an incredible coincidence, Bill died of a coronary at age thirty, and my coronary at that age revived all those memories and some of the anxieties.—M.R.

looking back into those memories, to be able to sort my feelings and distinguish between Mel's death and my own. And, if need be, I could take his death in stride. I knew he could die. I knew I would suffer a terrible loss. I knew he didn't want to die. I knew he was not abandoning me.

But there was that other set of feelings, at least equally powerful, which need to be distinguished: social pressure. When Bill died, I felt enormous social pressure. It had little to do with my life except that it was imposed on me and I was therefore forced to attend to it—to ward off its imposition. Bill's death came at a time when I had, in effect, just escaped from prison and was riding high on freedom. I was knocked off my props, but my drive for independence from authoritative imposition was so strong that I was able to stand firm against it.

From all directions came the pressures to do one thing or another in prescribed ways. It was my duty to have a funeral. Duty to whom? To our children? Family? Community? Me? Well, I was told, you know those rituals serve a purpose. How will we know Bill is dead if you don't follow tradition? Bill was gone from his body and there were all those people saying I should embalm his body to make it look to them as though he were still in it. So they could go through mumbo-jumbo which had nothing to do with anything Bill or I ever felt or wanted. And I should take food from my children's mouth to pay for all this! And I should take the children stage center with me before an audience curious to know our feelings. That would help our children? An audience telling themselves this is their way of sharing and easing *our* pain and helping us know our loss. Our pain and loss? Maybe theirs, but not mine or ours!

The children and I sat alone in the sun and began the only healing that really counts: accepting loss forthrightly and moving on as best one can. I trusted our friends—some

baffled by my rejection of ritual—to respect my choice.
My trust was well founded, and after the fact friends told
me they were glad to be able to remember Bill alive rather
than as a corpse.

1976 faded into 1977. Mel and I loved each other but
we knew there were deep changes. Mel clung to feeling
that I was abandoning him. I came to feel he was somehow
leaving me. Sometimes we tried to talk about what was
going on, but often those talks were punctuated with angry
arguments. We both felt shame and helplessness when we
found ourselves hurt or hurtful.

The struggles weren't just Mel's. I felt they stemmed
from his resistance to facing certain realities, quite as *he*
felt they were caused by my stance. There was no need to
attribute rightness or wrongness to either of us. Rather,
it just mattered that we could not readily make peace with
the issues at hand.

It was incredible to me that two people living together
so well and intimately for so many years still had significant areas in which they could not establish useful contact or make reliable readings. When I thought of all the
love, sophistication, intelligence, and motivation we
brought to our marriage, yet we still had communication
problems where we'd rather not, I couldn't wonder that
marriage breakdown was commonplace. Whatever success
couples—married or not—have in openly achieving common goals, it does seem to me that always one is acting
alone in some respects. That is, one must decide alone how
one will stand in relation to some commonality. Mel and I
were no exception. I could see my aloneness in our most
successful collaborative efforts; could see that each of us
had power always to interact toward the common goal or

not. I never fully understood Mel's opposition to my early planning for self-termination. But I can speak further of my own thinking and want to do so since somehow these considerations of mine feed into the complex fibers of my developing the Exit House concept.

It is a little awkward for me to do this (although easy in some respects) because I realize Mel must live with whatever I write. So with some caution and at the risk of oversimplifying, let me note a few personal reflections about personally confronting feelings of separation and/or death.

I approached each of my three marriages with a monogamous commitment, but I was at a different stage of development each time. Bill and I had a virginal marriage which was so short-lived that we barely fantasized about possible separation. We did speak of eventual death in some imagined distant time. I assumed in our old age. We had a little taste of fantasizing about separation when it appeared during World War II that fathers of two children would be drafted. Bill died before that could happen. But I remember keen distress at the thought, a sort of terror of separation. I wasn't at all afraid of being alone in the house or anything of that sort. Just fear of something happening to Bill which would leave me stranded and helpless. If he came home crippled, I could cope. But if he never came home, it was as though I'd be transformed into a nonentity.

Such reflections seem relevant to me when I try to comprehend some of the resistance I find others having about looking at death. Others seem to think of death only in relation to someone dying. Then, it seems to me, is about the least useful time to look at one's feelings. Why is there resistance to look at or speak of death in any meaningful, personal way when all is well? I suspect the key has to do with how a particular person has looked at and dealt with early separation experiences—particularly separation from parents. Much of our culture discourages separation, encouraging people to remain locked to family ties throughout adulthood, interpreting separation negatively as rejection rather than, say, a positive approach to respect.

My earliest sense of separation from my parents was psychological but nonetheless very real. While it was too largely an expression of feelings of rejection, there was sufficient love out of which our separation eventually came to be based on respect. I had been programmed to think I was irrelevant if I stood independent of another. That is, if separated. To be someone, I was expected to be bound always to parent or spouse. In this equation of separation there is a deeply ominous sense of being dead while yet alive. There is suffocating imagery of being buried alive, of having no power of your own by which to find and choose among alternatives. Separation equals helplessness, rejection, being stranded, trapped. These conditions add up to a dreadful sense of death being something fearsome. I imagine that one way of living with attachments which one feels one cannot live without must be to avoid recognition of dependence upon those attachments. That is, one must not allow oneself to consider one's separateness. While this may enable one to move along, it certainly leaves one terribly vulnerable if death overtakes the love object with whom one is so locked, upon whom one is dependent for one's own identification. Another way might be to offset fearsome images of death with heavenly images of a good personal life beyond death. But, as I noted during my childhood while observing behavior around deaths, there seems little indication of anyone being able to celebrate at death such a passage. At best, the bereaved is pressed to seek comfort in such images.

Finding myself as an independent person has taken most of my life. The task being ever so incomplete. Ironically, I found myself beginning to bear full fruit just in the approach to 1978. Ironically? Perhaps not. Perhaps we all have a potential for bearing fruit throughout our lives; sometimes the fruit of children and always the fruit of mind. Feeling independent, productive, and potentially relevant makes any day worth living! So, too, does the sense that one is able to approach those goals. For me, these possibilities are basic to a life of personally satisfying quality. And so too, for me, if these possibilities become remote, *impossible*, the day is not worth living. This is the "quality of life" control of which I speak. This is the basic premise upon which Exit House is founded. This is the reason—those possibilities no longer exist for me—that I am preparing for a rational suicide.

Standing by with Mel through his struggle with these ideas and beliefs made me extraordinarily mindful of just how far I had grown in my self-esteem and sufficiency. When it seemed Mel might find my life's interest so intolerably confronting that he might regard some fragile area of our relationship as an aperture to escape the pressure within the relationship, I did not feel compelled to turn my pain into a wiping out of myself. I understood for the first time that if Mel didn't want to be with me there was no call for me to discard my beliefs. In fact, my self-esteem and confidence in the validity of my beliefs had grown so strong that I was certain I could stand alone if need be. I still suffered unresolved inadequacies. I still harbored residual aversion to earning money (perhaps the equivalent of some men's aversion to sewing, ironing, bed-making, or rocking a baby). But in the area of our confrontation I could hold my ground. Not only could I withstand tests, I could also welcome them. It was terrific being able to say to myself earnestly that I would rather stand alone than sacrifice hard-earned convictions which, I believed, could serve others; or than lure Mel into staying in our relationship. Such thoughts may seem insignificant to others, but for me they were astonishing achievements. Particularly since I knew a break in our relationship would be staggering to us both and even to others.

During the summer of 1977 Mel and I structured a test for ourselves. Mel was as surprised as I. We decided, for the first time in our lives, to spend two months apart during the summer of 1978. We were shaken by our audacity and yet entirely loving and very serious. We planned that Mel would summer at a distance from our familiar territory—New York City and Cape Cod. I would stay at our comfortable home in the city, since I meant to devote the entire year to completing Exit House. By happenstance we had one lucky break. The summer house we loved and lived in for ten years would no longer be available to us. This forced a natural break from established summer patterns. But that was the only break.

We returned to the city that September of 1977, and I plunged into the pencil-sharpening phase of writing, clearing the agendas and such so as to free myself for a hard period of writing. Part of this task included helping Mel's daughter, Lisa, establish her first independent apartment. Recently I had done the same for my daughter, Timmy, and I wanted to do as much for Lisa. I worked with high efficiency, and was so close to finished that I rolled paper into the typewriter. Then, in October, the ogre of cancer decided my bloodline had been cancer-free long enough. It struck Timmy.

I say that losing our summer home was the only break, but I'm wrong. It was also a lucky break that I had severed my employment responsibilities. As a consequence, I could free my time for the terrible flurry of coming to grips with cancer's impact—being there for Timmy, seeing her through a mastectomy, researching and healing. My writing project was shelved through the holidays. Timmy's new life mattered more.

Fortunately, Timmy's prognosis was excellent after a simple mastectomy. By January 1978 Timmy was stable and had spiritedly resumed normal activities. Lisa was launched into her first professional job and her own apartment. Mel was doing very well in all respects except that he continued to be strained by internal struggle. I was back at the typewriter, plunging into the work, feeling good that at this time in my life I had such good confidence and work to offset the concern I felt for the future of our relationship and our individual selves. I felt proud that we dared test ourselves, and was well aware that most of my life I'd not have dared venture such separation from a spouse, however temporary, as was coming in July. The months leading to July felt emotionally important. There was a lessening of acrimony when we talked of our central issues.

In February 1978 I became sixty-one. How maligned is this age! I loved it! Onward, earthquakes and all!

Was I overconfident? I was still human and fallible and residually neurotic. For example, when I did routine self-examination of my breasts, I'd come to feel that my left breast's ordinary lumpiness felt somewhat abnormal. I told myself I must be overidentifying with Timmy's left-breast mastectomy. Surely in a family where there had been no cancer it was not reasonable to expect left-breast cancer in two generations at the same time. I decided I must be imagining the thickening of breast tissue. My fourth annual examination at the Guttman Institute, a breast research center, was due the next month. So, no need to act hastily.

Now we come to the *now* of my life span. A time that
holds me so close to my life's landscape that I have to
strain for objectivity of view.

On March 28, 1978, Mel was in San Francisco. The
beautiful spring day was in my step as I walked from the
bus to Guttman, even though my head was suddenly and
surprisingly flooded with a whole array of vivid fantasies.
My favorite vivid fantasy was cheerfully recounting to
Mel, when he returned in a week, how I approached this
Guttman appointment with absurd notions that I might
have cancer. I'd tell him how that absurd fantasy triggered
an assortment of other fantasies about how I would deal
with that. In this favorite fantasy, Guttman found no
problem.

In all the fantasies there was the assumption that whatever Guttman found, they would not tell me I had cancer,
even if they were certain of it. Instead, they would flat-
facedly advise me of the presence of abnormal tissue
which, they'd hasten to say, might be benign; I should consult my family doctor. I was certain I'd feel annoyed by
such delay, resent their withholding their opinion, however much more testing would be indicated. And I'd feel
frustrated, with a sense of urgency to be examined by
another doctor, particularly since I knew I would not be
able to reach my regular doctor immediately. So I was
feeling anger as I bounced along, approaching the
Guttman Institute.

In my fantasies, of course, I jumped simultaneously to
the worst possibilities as well as to the images of laughing
at my own foolishness. So it was, as I strode through the
balmy sunny day, that I saw in remarkable detail the
entire scenario of what actually evolved. I knew before I
entered the building exactly what my reactions would be
if it turned out that I had a tumor. I realized I would feel

deeply distressed and want Mel's comfort. At the same time, I already knew from our other growing pains that I was capable of coping alone. If I turned to Mel for comfort, it unquestionably would be beautifully forthcoming. On the other hand, if I turned to him for comfort through however long it would take to evaluate a tumor, then there would be essentially no way to separate myself from him for independent determination of what to do if the tumor proved to be malignant.

Still walking, I concluded that at least I wanted *not* to involve Mel in the coping unless/until malignancy was established. And then? If that? My heart skipped a beat at the thought. On the stage in my mind's eye I saw myself collapsed into Mel's arms, outdoing even Sarah Bernhardt. We were in a heap in the glaring spotlight, whose heat burned as though the sun had turned itself on too high.

Fantasy raced. Suppose I do have cancer! And Mel would know? Well, no way would he go off for his separate summer. And would that make me feel better? Certainly, and in some important ways. But the thought of Mel's staying home because I had cancer, rather than because he had tested himself and found he wanted to continue our relationship regardless of my life-ending plan, was upsetting. Completing our test was more important than not completing it because I had cancer. Even if I had cancer, I'd rather cope by myself than in a relationship marked by entrapment. If it turned out that I had cancer, I decided I would do what I could to conceal it from Mel until after his trip. After that, we'd both be more clear and emotionally able to cope. I'd rather give myself the benefit of that than the benefit of quick comfort. I wanted not to tell Mel even more than I terribly much wanted to tell him. I wanted to feel and trust my own capability. I knew its loving base.

If I have a tumor, will it be like Timmy's? That was
the first question that sprang to mind. If so, I supposed
I would have to have surgery to determine with certainty
whether it was cancerous. If it proved benign, then I could
tell Mel what a close call we had, and we could laugh
about my hardheaded independence and get on with our
lives. If it proved malignant? Then . . .

I saw myself having two courses. One duplicated
Timmy's. I'd be advised to have a mastectomy on the
grounds of probability of removing all malignancy and so
enabling a normal life span. If it came to that, I knew I'd
have relatively little difficulty taking that trauma in stride.
I'd seen Timmy do it and knew I could do it more easily
simply for having gone through her experience with her.
Of course, if I had to have a mastectomy before summer,
there'd be no possibility of concealment from Mel. But at
least I could try alone to get through the process of learning whether it was malignant.

Suppose it is malignant and the odds are against a
mastectomy salvaging my life span? I'd be grateful to
know Exit House so well! I would never turn the remaining portion of my life span into a state of existing for the
sake of waiting for terminal ravages or of focusing on a
search against odds for cures, remissions, or life extensions.
Let others be free and aided to follow such courses of
choice. Not I! I would make the best calculation possible
as to how long I could live with emotional and physical
comfort which, as measured by myself, I would regard
as adequate. I would plan to end my life at the end of
that period and so make it possible to devote the remainder
of my life to fullest living. Under those circumstances, I
assumed my shortened life would rule out the possibility
of our test. We would have to replace our separate-summer
test with the test of whether we could use our relationship
to help me end my life and launch him into a new one.

The walk from the bus to Guttman was a mere two blocks, yet all those fantasies burst forth. As I walked into the building, I still clung to the fantasy of laughing with Mel about the head trip I'd made on this walk. But I knew myself unequivocally. My course was clear.

Guttman's confirmation of the tumor's presence was as exasperating as I had known it would be. Exasperating? Outrageous! The shuffle searching for doctors was frustrating, although quickly resolved. My selected surgeon braved sharing his pretesting impression that I was not only malignant but that my malignancy was quite advanced. By at least two years!

I went in for the operation on April 14, never telling Mel or anyone else. I made the decision that they could not perform the mastectomy, no matter what was found. The doctor agreed that I could opt for treatment and said I might figure out a way to conceal it from Mel. He volunteered that I would not lose my hair, but I might feel groggy for a day or two at a time. The primary tumor was removed and was malignant.

My cancer proved to be significantly advanced. The odds were very high against salvaging my normal life span. Mastectomy was pointless. The calculations, in spring 1978, were that I could count on one to two decent years.

I set out to make the best of it. It was enormously difficult and enormously rewarding to have come to this point by myself. Furthermore, it looked as if I could have my cake and eat it too! Mel and the rest of the family remained ignorant of my physical plight. (I told them I was in Boston the weekend of my operation.) If I'd been able to keep it under wraps this well and this long, I thought, perhaps I could salvage our relationship test. That would greatly enrich these final months. For both of us, I believed.

The best-laid plans do indeed go awry. I realize it is awfully difficult for anyone to comprehend that for three months, including surgery, I could keep my family in the dark. However, I did that. Thanks to the very full lives we customarily led, I might have carried through until July. Thanks to the debilitation of chemotherapy, I failed. Chemotherapy is physically debilitating and emotionally oppressive, and its effects—despite my herculean effort to conceal them—became evident to Mel. Even that might not have disrupted my plan had not Mel, on June 16, 1978, declared he felt I was excluding him from my life. That did it! I couldn't bear his going off with such an utterly mistaken view of me.

I came to the end of the only secret I had ever kept from Mel.

I began keeping an extensive journal, writing as often as possible, immediately upon learning I would have to undergo tests for cancer. I wanted to keep an accurate record of my physical and emotional responses for my own use and understanding as well as for Mel's, though he did not know I was keeping such a journal until April 1979—obviously, or he would have known I had cancer. For the purposes of this book, I would like now to draw from my journal, to backtrack chronologically to April 1978. The following notes should help to explain whatever is yet unexplained about my cancer, my relationship with those I love, and the approaching Exit date.

April 3, 1978: My view after six days of living alone with awareness that I probably have breast cancer.

All that follows needs to be understood within the privacy framework clarified in the accompanying To

Whom It May Concern statement. Also, assuming that I really do have cancer and that it may have metastasized or not.

1. I want to get myself into the care of a good oncologist who is specialized in breast cancer surgery.

2. I believe the next best step is for various tests and scanning. The sooner the better. Is hospitalization necessary for this? How long? Where? When?

3. After step 2 (above), I gather that a biopsy will probably be needed and that hospitalization may not be necessary for this. If hospitalization is necessary, I'd just as soon couple it with step 2, if practical. Immediate hormonal assay is indicated, I believe. If biopsy reveals metastases or reason not to have a mastectomy, then I want to proceed with arrangements without informing my friends. I assume hospitalization, if any, would be terminated at this point.

4. Following step 3 (biopsy), if mastectomy is advised, I definitely want time outside of the operating room for alert weighing of my alternatives. Assuming I'd probably want to accept the recommendation, I would, then, also need time to inform my husband. I will gladly agree to a mastectomy if I conclude it is the best course for me. But I would not want a Halsted.

TO WHOM IT MAY CONCERN: April 1978

As you participate with me in clarifying and weighing the decisions immediately at hand regarding my probable breast cancer will you please accept from the outset that I have private personal need to prevent all persons—other than you who are professionally involved—from knowing about my condition. I ask you to give me the courtesy of not questioning my reason. As you aid me, I would appreciate the benefit of your highest sense of professional confidence.

You should know that at present not even my husband, family, or any friend is informed. Of course, at some point it will be necessary to inform certain persons. It is extremely important that it be I, alone, who determines whom and when.

Since you do not know me, you might reasonably question whether my exceptional concern for privacy reflects some inner turmoil which could disturb my medical course. If so, please tell me and I will arrange for you to speak with a psychiatrist who knows me well enough to vouch for my stability. If you feel concern that beneath my special need for privacy there lurks undue fear of surgery, breast loss, or some sort of troublesome denial mechanism, please tell me and let me try to reassure you directly that this is not the case. I've a substantial history of being an open person who deals directly and well with adversity. I will this time, too—particularly if you will share the keeping of our confidential relationship.

JO ROMAN

Temporary address to be used for all correspondence and contact.
% Incheck
348 E. ——th St.
NYC 10003
Tel: 555-9773

April 9, 1978: 13th day since tumor confirmed. Death is not at all frightening. But loss of life quality is dreadful. So the goal is to fight not to preserve a breast or even avoid death. Rather, the fight is to preserve/create a qualitatively desirable life. To "die awake"!

April 11, 1978: 4:30 P.M. In an hour or so Mel and Timmy
will be here for supper and eve. I'm restless. Last days have
been quite tear-free and deliciously regarding, enlighten-
ing, and so goodness-filled. Today's tension is triggered by
the reality of breast surgery pressing in upon me, triggered
by today's painless (except for time consumption and the
drag of trekking up to CPH) bone scan.

Later: Queasy. Weepy. Even though I treated myself
to a good cry this afternoon. Heretofore, such a cry was
very effective. Even when I'd slip into fantasies of matters
being worse than I really believe they are. E.G. noticing
that my shins ache and wondering about bone cancer.
Suspect my mood is due not only to above but, also, to
awareness that soon—tomorrow—I must prepare a letter
for Mel to cover the unlikely possibility that I'll not survive surgery. (Bill only went in for a hernia operation!)
It breaks me up thinking I must write such a letter. But,
to the marrow of my bones, I know my decision not to tell
Mel is the best and gutsiest decision of my life. At any rate,
in these thoughts is awareness that my physical machinery
isn't quite as sturdy as it has been for past surgery. Never
before did I have thought of not surviving. This time, no
doubt because I'm somewhat bugged by the notion of
cancer as a rampant destructive force now abiding in me,
I have feelings that my heart isn't as strong as it used to
be. Too much fat, I daresay! And, blood pressure?

Must stop for now . . .

April 17, 1978: 5:30 P.M. An hour or so to write before
going to meet Mel for dinner. Circumstances and moods
are in such a state of ready-shift. Walking from 96th Street
station on Central Park West I was so happy to be heading
home. I felt exhilarated . . . like skipping or singing. I kept

telling myself, "Jo Roman, you have cancer and if you behaved as most people would your life would be very very different right now. You'd not be free to travel home on the subway by yourself, feeling good and grinning. Mel and Timmy and all your friends would be feeling rotten and giving you their love in form of 'stiff upper lip . . . you're terrific . . . and maybe they'll be able to cure you . . . they do such great things nowadays.' And everything they'd say—in addition to things I'd say—would be loaded with multiple meanings. And everyone would be calling each other and feeling awful for me . . . and especially for Mel and Timmy . . . and each other. Mel would be struggling to hold himself together and researching and trying to pick me up at the hospital and kicking himself for all the human condition he suffers and can't make vanish just because I'm sick. (Had to pause before writing "I'm sick." I feel so well. And my fingers wanted to type "because I'm going to be sick.") At any rate, we'd be all mucked up and there's something really crazy about that. Why should the ones closest and lovingest be cut off by craziness at such a time? I realize one could hardly expect anyone to clap their hands with glee. And I, myself, don't see alternatives other than the one I've taken. And I can't say enough how much in love I am with my decision to keep my cancer secret as long as possible; how incredibly lucky I feel to have the strength—so far—to get me over the sinking spots; how super that my closest ones will be so very there to help share any burden too heavy for me and that I'll be able to help them with theirs, too.

May 1, 1978: Nowadays I seldom finish writing anything I start if it's connected with my cancer trip. The normal part of my life keeps interrupting. It's such a nuisance having to carefully tuck away secret material whenever and wherever Mel or Timmy might be.

My optimism about taking chemotherapy in secret stride still holds but admittedly is a bit shaky. Most waves of nausea have occurred when I'm alone and were easy enough to deal with, but when I get queasy with people around I feel anxious and go for the antinausea pills faster than I'd like. Alone, I never take them because I can ride out the bouts and am eager to know just what they are.

My incision is so fantastic that I don't even bother keeping myself covered and/or turned away from Mel's view now. Ain't that sumpin! Felt my axillary tumor this A.M.—interestingly, I'm little inclined to keep checking it, perhaps because it isn't easy to do—and it actually seems smaller. Wishful? But my breast feels more sore now than in the days right after surgery. Will rap that out tomorrow and Wednesday with doctors.

Have notice from dentist that it's time for my periodic exam. Strange sensation of wondering whether to follow through while time, energy, and dollars are in shortening supply. Imagine I will follow through before long. It'd be nice at least to have a cleaning. Just can't tolerate working in another appointment right now.

June 4, 1978: Feel I just must try to squeeze in some notes. Last Friday was the tenth day of the current fourteen-day chemo stretch. When, that morning, I reached for my chemo pills, I simply found I could not take them. I hadn't been thinking about not taking them. I just could not. I'd been feeling not significantly more queasy on this stretch than previously unless, perhaps, on Thursday. Just feeling worn by the relentless strain and, so, having less endurance. Whatever, I just couldn't get myself to take them.

I felt bewildered. Still do, but less so now, even though I've no comprehension of the relevance of my action. I haven't taken any pills since last Thursday morning. Today, for the first time since Thursday I'm feeling reasonably okay without just pretending or overriding my feelings. I feel not *well*, but relatively almost well. I don't feel I've done myself wrong by stopping and suppose I will be resuming eventually. Maybe tomorrow?

On Friday, when I held those pills, frozen, I was sure that if I took them I would be so sick that I would not be able to conceal. Even if I didn't say cancer, no casual explanation would satisfy Mel or Timmy. It would be so uncharacteristic of me to be as sick as I felt I verged on being. Some breakdown seemed threatening. I suspect M & T are noticing that I'm less energetic nowadays . . . am exhausted evenings, go to bed early, etc. I see "a look" in Mel's eye. I've developed a strange cough and head drainage—not a cold and not, seemingly, an allergic reaction to something in the air—and I've been "blaming" that. But I was at some edge I felt I must not cross. I was/am quite willing to sacrifice time for quality.

Even without the pills on Friday I felt awfully on edge all morning, wondering whether I should have canceled my appointment. I feared I might not be able to go through an interview. I felt like I might start vomiting midway. Or faint? Or diarrhea? Or just cry uncontrollably?

Timmy is moving into the neighborhood and at some level she must be aware and puzzled about my not being involved as I'd ordinarily be. So frustrating!

Later: Nowadays, I find myself having a running series of internal dialogues. At least once a day I come very very close to telling Mel. Always at moments when I'm feeling most strained and fearful that I can't sustain the secret.

Godfrey! How close I come! Or to telling Timmy. Sometimes I think I'm about to blurt it out. I find myself re-
hearsing, sort of, what I would say. Then I see their faces.
That hurts, true. Sure no shortage of tears. Then a period
of aghastness over the unknowing time. Time to reconstruct
it all for comprehension. That task alleviates what I
imagine would be a period of oversolicitousness from
family. But then comes the time when the essential emot-
ing has run its course and one arrives at sheer waiting.

June 21, 1978: Home from PH, starting my third twenty-
eight-day cycle of chemotherapy with Dr. ————————.
Still friendly in manner, he nevertheless is distinctly different with me now. More guarded, somewhat ill at ease,
signaling the need to hurry on.

Told him I'd skipped the last few days of chemo and am
considering discontinuing. He had difficulty looking me in
the eye and said—seemingly from a textbook—that the
choice is mine, but that, of course, chemo is what I should
do. And, that if I didn't continue chemo I'd risk "getting
cancer again." The latter comment really bugged me. It's
the second time he's done that to me—implied that I'm
probably cancer-free. This time, too, I noted that he
seemed to be implying I am cancer-free . . . isn't it so that
I have a malignancy now? He phumps and says, well yes.
I feel he has somehow tried to mislead me away from
reality into some sort of false optimism. I feel he's ac-
customed to patients who compliantly stiff-upperlip it or
who fret and aren't inclined to question his judgment. And
he senses I'm some unfamiliar type. I find myself protecting him, being careful to keep the firmness of my query
from frightening him. More because I really need to elicit
for myself some more useful communication than out of

indulgence of him. Still, this is not the rapport I'd like to have now.

I came around the issues still another way, trying to give him an opening to tell me what I want and feel entitled to know. I said I hadn't gathered any information that led me to feel that if I discontinued chemo that I should expect discomfort during, say, the next twelve months. Whereas, on chemo, twelve months is qualitatively reduced to approximately three months. (Figuring half time nausea and the remaining half time reduced by the pileup of work during the nausea weeks. So, I end up with about one quarter good time and three quarters discomfort and relentless preoccupation with cancer.) He seemed unable to come up with anything to disabuse me of my view. Commented that cancer might grow and spread during that time. I said I understood that. And it seemed he didn't want further discussion.

He asked re symptoms. I told him of continued bowel question, vaginal burn, mouth sore, queasiness when not taking Cytoxan, two-week cough sans cold, and one day's ankle swelling. He examined me and indicated these things all happenstance and no cause for concern and unrelated to chemo. Blood pressure now good: 155 over 90.

June 22, 1978: 8:55 A.M. Tears wetting my face, my upper lip must be wiped, my chest is clogged with sobs. Mel has just gone off in search of space so open and yet private that he can dare unleash and explore his own congestion.

It's funny how just the struggle to transform feelings into words on a page cools the emotions even though the words barely reflect the pool from which they've been drawn. Tears have simply evaporated.

And now I can feel enough distance from the emotions

of a few moments ago to look back upon them and seek comprehension and direction by approaching them from this different angle.

I walked from saying good-bye to Mel at the door, back into the lovely light of our bathroom, and *forced* myself to take Cytoxan. And there came an engulfing sense of familiarity with a facet of this life drama. It's one thing to question my undergoing chemotherapy and sensibly collecting available information upon which I can act with informed judgment. It's something quite else to deal with feelings which press from inside against the accumulating information. Feels like I've been in this bloody place so many tiresome times! I could take today's pills only by forcing them down while suddenly being flooded with a sea of memories of probably saving lives precious to me by struggling to a stand against authoritative advice/pressure. Suddenly I feel I'm again engaged in such a struggle.

A half-hour to get that last paragraph out! And now? Here at 9:40 . . . into the day feeling I've got myself reasonably together. Feel happiness and confidence in Mel's actively going off to commune with himself. Onward . . .

June 26, 1978: Tuesday. Mel's last day of being fifty. An especially clarifying morning meeting jointly with Dr. —————. Last week I sent him note revealing that Mel is now sharing the load with me.

My bottom line is quite as I had deduced from previous medical sessions and reading but significantly more clear. Skipping all the inevitable qualifications, it boils down to high probability that I can count on one good year. "Good"? Well, even without chemotherapy I *might* not get physically uncomfortable as my cancer does whatever it's inclined to do. With chemotherapy, probably my discom-

fort would be limited to the side effects of the chemotherapy. Present chemotherapy discomfort reduces my
comfort/efficiency level to, let's say, half time. It might
buy me half time for a second year. My response to that is
that I'd like to consider gambling on skipping the chemo
entirely and having a good full year up front rather than
having two good half-time years with chemotherapy
stretched across them. Dr. ——————— counters with a
compromise, to continue—more comfortable than now—
and strengthen possibility of a second year closer to a
probability. Third year? Maybe. Maybe with a fight for it.
But I doubt that I want to put up that fight. I'd rather put
my focus and energy into this year. Next could be a bonus.
And from here that much seems a beautiful sufficiency.
Even though there's so much to do! With this clarity and
Mel's knowing/sharing, I'm almost ready to swing into a
home run. Soon as I get over the next agonizing hurdle,
telling dear Timmy and seeing her through to stability.

September 10, 1978: All that stuff was yesterday. Today's
not so up. Yesterday's up was enhanced by my skipping my
Cytoxan dose. But today I'm back on it and what a shitty
difference it makes. The pressing nausea edge, the welling
tears, a backache triggering fear of some sudden "premature" cancer quirk shortening the shortened life I've made
peace with. The cleanup of last night's debris. And feeling
a whole morning being consumed by thingyness. Into the
afternoon. Struggling for composure. Relieved when Mel
comes in and lets me dump on his shoulder for a moment.
More struggle for another sort of balance. So painful knowing that my relieving myself with Mel is sometimes at
painful expense to him. The work load he carries while
he's coping with his own emotional turmoil is so heavy that

often it is less painful to me to struggle along than to spill on him. Can't always control my leanings. Still . . .

October 5, 1978: Yesterday proved to be a total wipeout. Couldn't get out of bed to get to work. Nausea, aching.

Maybe today, after Mel gets off for Arizona and chores are out of the way, maybe my bile will stay low enough so I can work.

November 1, 1978: 221 more days . . . Reflecting . . .

December 21, 1978: Last night, I lost control of my bowels while I slept. I woke up with shit in the bed. Possibly it was a seizure—breast tumors can spread to the brain. My back pains have been so great lately that I have needed help putting my shoes on. The cancer is spreading. I am terrified I may have a seizure in the street. Or in a restaurant. Or someone's home. So I am writing a letter—just in case.

February 6, 1979: I'm into a reflective pause to catch my breath from the eventful last days and, hopefully, to find and set my bearings for the next hundred or so days. Days which seem to me to be my penultimate time. The time in which projects and all but the most intimate and a few practical relationships must be drawn to a close. A time which I feel impatient to plunge into, yet I know I must first tend to transitioning and the ever relentless intrusive practicalities. Another tooth has broken—the third since chemotherapy: related?—and I must go off for repairs before my tongue is shredded.

How to finish my will? How to bring this apartment into its own stride? Ooooh the stacks of papers. Lisa? Am I going to be forced to include her in the terrible pile of people and projects and things I must be forced to abandon with a sense of unnecessary failure? Unnecessary, except for time shortage? Who else? What else? Somehow, in these next days I must make such decisions. Part of the pain will be casting off treasures for the sake, hopefully, of salvaging resources for the final stretch. Exit House. Sculpture. Mel. The incredible separation of myself from my flesh and those extensions of it who are—as family and friends—so deeply me.

I am in tears and must stop the flow so I can make my way to the dentist. I turn from the typewriter for tissues . . . turn into sun falling across Liz Levin's so sweet daffodils and Barbara Rousso's fragrant spring flowers right onto Mom Roman's dear smile and Timmy's cracked-up laughter all framed in that assortment of memorabilia and usefulnesses which surrounds the spot where Mel and I have shared so many meals with each other and friends for the past decade—but where we rarely have time nowadays. Love and the ticking of a meter fills all space and follows wherever I go.

March 1979: Coming up with creative ideas for gifts for someone who is dying is a neat trick. One I'm savoring! Sari got me at Xmas by putting together a collection of yummies I'd not otherwise dare eat. Now, Mel has come up with a knockout gift for me on our twentieth anniversary. Imagine having personalized stationery made up for a dying person! He did it! True, he knew I'm planning to prepare a letter for mailing to one and all when I die; but who else would have dreamed up this super-stationery ! ! !

May 22, 1979: I have finished the draft of my obituary, to be placed in the Lancaster newspaper, *The New Era.*

FORMER RESIDENT OF LANCASTER, PA. DIES IN NEW YORK CITY

Jo Roman lived 62 full and varied years; 15 of them in Lancaster as Mary Clodfelter, and then as Mary Jo Wade. When widowed in 1943 she moved to Alaska with her son, Tom, and her daughter, Timmy. She attended Lancaster schools and graduated from Millersville State Teacher's College in 1938. Later she did graduate work in psychology at the University of North Carolina and earned a Master's Degree in psychiatric social work at Adelphi University in New York. Her life interests gathered around art and human dynamics.

Across the past decade or so she developed keen interest in the possible use of suicide as a rational creative means of enriching life with a good death. She came to believe such options must be developed now that lives can be extended against one's wish. If we do not want to risk being locked into unwanted existence against our will to live, then, Ms. Roman believed, we must recognize and respect the right of people to end their lives responsibly.

Ms. Roman's beliefs were well known to her family and friends, and they formed a supportive circle around her when some 15 months ago it was discovered she had advanced cancer. She opted then not to spend the remainder of her life fighting against odds to extend her life. Over 100 people participated in helping her to live fully, to minimize medical treatment, and to bring her life to an end which both she and they could respect.

During her last months, Ms. Roman completed a manuscript (its working title is *Exit House*), a life sculpture, and material for an educational film based on videotapes which show her family and friends coming to grips with her philosophy.

Jo Roman gently ended her life at her home in New York City on June 10, 1979. She is survived by her husband, Dr. Mel Roman, professor of psychiatry at Albert Einstein College of Medicine; daughter Timmy Ehrhart; stepdaughter Lisa Roman, all of New York City. Her son, daughter-in-law, and two granddaughters—Thomas, Joanne, and Melanie and Valerie, respectively—live in Harrisburg, Pa. A brother, Fred, lives in Arizona. In Lancaster she is survived by her brother John and her mother Adeline Lawrence Clodfelter. Her late father was the Rev. Charles W. Clodfelter.

June 1, 1979: Timmy and Mel have grown increasingly at peace, I believe and feel, with my dying. They seem to have all their resources and support systems mobilized. So, however much the amputation may pain and bleed, I trust their recovery will be as deep and swift as possible.

June 8, 1979: Evening. 9 o'clock. I'm trying to organize and assemble the elements—or an assortment of same—of my life to pack tomorrow into the pine trunk, even at this hour, being built in the studio.

I must get on with the assembly of life material. How ridiculous so many of the elements. And how remarkably they add up.

III

FROM THE
LANDSCAPE
OF YOUR LIFE

Means and Rights

I aim to bring my life to a relatively swift, irreversible, and utterly painless end by ingesting a lethal dose of Seconal. I expect to be enveloped in sweet sleep within twenty minutes, and then dead within three hours.

To protect myself against regurgitation, which might result from rapid intake of an inordinate amount of water while swallowing forty-five capsules of 100-mg size—i.e., 4500 mg of Seconal—I plan to take a 10-mg tablet of Compazine—a nausea suppressant— every three hours for twelve hours preceding the Seconal.*

To accelerate absorption of the Seconal and to note the peace of death and the ongoing challenge of life, I will drink a champagne toast.

Do I have confidence in the effectiveness of my plan? How did I reach it? How did I acquire the drugs? Might the plan abort? Would I recommend the plan for others? Could others obtain the means? Are there alternatives? Questions flow on.

If one's goal is swift, painless, irreversible death, I know

---

* In the end she decided this was not necessary, as she planned to take the Seconal slowly, five to seven capsules at a time.—M.R.

of no better alternative within reach of laypersons. I gather that there are swifter means via intravenous or intramuscular injections. However, these generally are not obtainable without legal risk to the provider. Further, they are not painless.

It occurred to me that the people most likely to have done the best research for the purpose of developing an ideal means of self-terminating life would be located in government agencies such as the CIA or NASA. I wrote NASA saying that I assumed the USA would not be so heartless as to catapult astronauts into outer space prior to development of a retrieval system (even if the chance of an aborted mission was remote) without having equipped them with a means of self-termination. I asked whether they had provided reasonable means of self-termination. They replied they never considered such an eventuality. I didn't repeat my inquiry with the CIA. However, an inside informant did confirm CIA possession of a highly sophisticated glass canister which, when broken in the mouth, would release a fast-acting gas—strychnine-like—which would result in instant death. None was available for me and I was satisfied with that because I prefer sweet sleep to even a split second of glass crunched in my mouth or to convulsion. Perhaps the experts know something I don't.

How does one acquire 4500 mg of Seconal? My guess is that the average person might find it impossible. Doctors are, I believe, increasingly reluctant to prescribe Seconal. Perhaps especially if asked for it. Generally it is prescribed as a sedative for people with sleep problems. Perhaps twenty 50-mg capsules, not renewable. At that rate, if one's doctor would prescribe it at all, one would need to visit the doctor and elicit the prescription four times to accumulate 4500 mg. This procedure is costly in terms of time as well as money. And very unreliable for the average person. If you can convince your doctor that you have insomnia—and you might well be reluctant to lie—a non-narcotic drug such as Placidyl might be prescribed instead, and who knows whether that has a lethal potential? I hear there is a black market for Seconal. But many of the people I know wouldn't have the foggiest notion about how to tap that. I could but haven't. If I did, I think I'd have questions in my mind as to the quality of what I'd have purchased. And then no ready way to have its quality evaluated.

I occasionally do have a sleepless night and have found Seconal more effective than other sedatives. I have so informed my doctors and they have been willing to prescribe Seconal for me. I have specified that I prefer taking one 100-mg capsule to two 50-mg capsules. All true. Thus have I acquired my supply, in part. The supply from prescription has been supplemented by friends who voluntarily offered me Seconal from their own stock when they learned of my need. Here again do I see the value of sharing suicide reflections with others, especially *before* one has reason to commit suicide.

Many suicide attempts which are made with drugs fail because of inadequate dosage. The "Prediction of Suicide's Toxicity" chart, which can be found in medical reference books, lists the minimum lethal dose for numerous commonly available drugs. For Seconal it is 1.5 grams—that would be a little more than ten 100-mg capsules—and considerably less than I intend to take. I have been advised that while 1000 mg might indeed end one's life, its lethality is marginal. Even if there was no interference such as stomach pumping or regurgitation, instead of dying one might just sleep for twenty-four hours or so and wake up with nothing worse than a hangover. 2000 mg, I've been informed, is more certain to cause death but possibly not for many hours. Consequently, one would greatly increase the risk of discovery and interference. Additionally, in the event of revival, this dosage significantly increases the risk of brain damage. 3500 mg is the magic dosage with which, I'm told by an established medical doctor, one might count on irreversible death. In my plan—having lived through the revival by medical intervention of a friend who took a dose of another drug five times larger than anyone had been known to survive—I aim for at least an hour to pass before any medical personnel can get near my body.

Why am I taking 4500 mg rather than 3500 mg? Simply because one doctor consulted thought it a good safety measure and because I have that amount. If I have more and am able to take them, I will do so. If I were not concerned for the comfort of others, personally I'd be pleased to know that no revival team would have access to my body for a far longer period—say, twenty-four hours. My belief is that I will be gently asleep within twenty minutes, soon after dead, and that any revival before that would have me so brain-damaged that only a vegetable state could be maintained. I like to think that if that would happen that I would be beyond conscious awareness of my environment. I hate to think that my family and society might be burdened with such maintenance.

What if I didn't know about Seconal, or know the proper dosage, or have a prescription, or weren't able to afford its purchase? (In 1979 a 100-mg capsule of Seconal costs about twelve cents.) What if I didn't have any doctor friends? Is there any alternative means of suicide which would not hurt me, would be reasonably swift and irreversible? Alas! No information I've found holds such promise. I assume there are other drugs which would be as painless and effective as Seconal, but I don't know what they are, what quantities are effective, nor how to obtain them. So far as I can see, any suicide alternative other than an ingested drug includes some physical discomfort.

If some degree of physical discomfort must be resorted to, I gather that inhaling carbon monoxide is relatively painless. It is, of course, awkward, difficult to secure adequate privacy, potentially dangerous to others, and, if bungled, likely to leave one brain-damaged. I know of someone who thinks of drowning if a suitable drug isn't available when she eventually would end her life. I suppose that is relatively painless, but its suffocation would horrify me. I believe that there is no readily available decent alternative and none in sight. Surely there could and should be. Therefore I believe even people who wish to leave life gently and are not at all interested in self-murder are being forced by irrational societal attitudes to subject themselves to unconscionable torments—either of the ravages of old age and terminal illness or else of painful suicides of desperation.

I can still hear in my mind the voice and I can still look into the eyes of Jochen Seidel—after his twice being forced back from earnest suicide attempts into a spent life—telling me how much he did not want to hurt himself. He stared long from his fifth-floor window, wanting to die but not wanting to jump and hurt himself. Then he hung his body from a rafter, and everyone shuddered at his "bizarreness." His? Society's! I've read that hanging is, indeed, a swift, relatively painless, and generally irreversible means. But I would loathe being brought to that by a society that has the easy capacity to let me have a way to leave life in a gentle decent manner. When I think of how extremely difficult it is to commit suicide except by resorting to ugly means, I can't help but attribute much of our general recoil to suicide to this fact.

In my search across the years for an ideal Exit Pill—

swift, painless, irreversible—I learned some interesting things, but obviously discovered no means of exit better than the one I plan. Family, friends, and I have a broad range of associates in medical and related fields. Most now have been approached on the subject, and of course I've probed the literature.

One of the most useful facts I garnered is that, contrary to common belief, physicians do not know how best to end a life. They are focused on counteracting life-ending drugs and acts. So, although many respond to my initial queries thinking that they are well informed about means of suicide, in fact I found them to be very ill informed.

Whenever I could use rapport with a physician to make a comfortable inquiry, the physician initially would assume he or she would know the best way to commit suicide. Most commonly, they said they would take a lethal overdose of a generally unavailable drug such as morphine and that they probably would inject themselves. In all these discussions I made no exploration of what reasons they could imagine for precipitating such an act but often their fantasies seemed to be of terminal illness or intractable pain. No doctor I spoke with seemed abnormal, pathological, or suicidal. In fact, most were guarded against our discussions and opened up only cautiously. Their caution seemed specifically a concerned measurement of my interest rather than a concealment of their own views. Physicians have a suicide rate three times higher than the general population, according to Jacques Choron (*Suicide*, Scribner's, 1972).

Whenever physicians tried to provide me with useful references, they could not do better than refer me to the "Prediction of Suicide's Toxicity" chart, which gives information for about thirty toxic drugs frequently used in suicide attempts (Seconal is among them). But to note the commonly used drugs is to note only what drugs people are able to get their hands on and says naught of whether even one of these drugs is an ideal drug for suicide. One might just as well examine a chart of thirty most frequently used suicide methods. There (Choron, page 39) one can learn that in one year "sleeping pills and other pharmaceuticals" were used in only 12.4 percent of means whereas "firearms and explosives" rated 47.6 percent. But these figures tell us nothing of what means would have been ideal or preferred.

Surely availability of a scientifically developed Exit Pill which would assure ideally swift, painless, and irreversible death would essentially eradicate the use of the infinite list of alternative suicide means. A person deciding to end his or her life could do so respectfully and with dignity and would not be forced to desperate means. We could practically close the door on leaps from high ledges, slashings, drownings, gassings, poisonings, starvings, shootings. One might look for a significant reduction in vehicular "accidents" and their terrible toll on bystanders.

If an Exit Pill were available, would the number of suicides increase, decrease, or stay the same? Of course, no one can know. Nor could there be a certain measure, given the fact that existing suicide statistics are unquestionably understated and speculative at best. My own guess is that, in contrast to the unknown actual suicide rate, ready availability of an Exit Pill would significantly lower the suicide rate. The Exit Pill's availability would heighten each human being's sense of safety and freedom from unwanted and forced life, would heighten each person's sense of the mortal self and its attached rights and responsibilities.

There might well be a temporary increased rate among certain portions of the population: those patients in de-

pendent conditions and monitored against the possibility
of suicide, and some of the institutionalized aged, terminally ill, or life imprisoned. But, even in this essentially
entrapped population, I'd be surprised to find a massive
elected exodus from life. Much of this population has been
programmed to regard suicide as a stigma. Also, they may
have entrenched convictions of value in clinging to life
against all odds. Many of them, as well, would simply
make different judgments than I would about their life's
quality and their possible options.

As I write, my friend Bonnie cradles her dying mother,
my friend Patti cradles her dying father, my friend Kees
his dying wife, and my own mother shrivels in a nursing
home. We tell ourselves or are told "they cling to life" as
though we believe they treasure their drawn-out dying.
Perhaps so. Then why have we not given them the alternative of an Exit Pill?

To those who would protest development of an Exit Pill
and its ready availability, I would like to suggest that their
protest energies be directed instead to educating the public to see the relevance of its right to determine whether
powerful organizations may pollute our common air and
water supplies; to understand the risks of developing
nuclear energy; to appreciate the impact of product pro-
motion by tobacco and alcohol industries; to note the impact of ready access to guns and powerful motor vehicles.
I would like to state that I would join forces with all who
would develop education about and protection against
the abusive use of Exit Pills, as well as tobacco, alcohol,
guns, cars. I would join with all who would support the
sensible use of whatever products exist. I would support
education and protection of children from being abused
by misuse of any product on the market—including unnecessarily dangerous toys. I would especially join forces

with anyone who would protest air and water pollution by our industrial and governmental giants. I would even go so far as to join the so-called Right to Life forces to the extent that they do not presume to play God and, so, grant each person the right to die as well as the right to live in accordance with her own values. I would ask that we share the task of finding ways to help those unable to make their own decisions, and for those directly responsible for them to be given the protected right and responsibility to act in their behalf.

I suppose I must acknowledge and accept the right of persons to end their lives by means other than that which I consider ideal. I like to think that most people would not want to inflict pain upon themselves, but I know that what is pain to one person is not to another. I also realize that people are enormously inventive and individualistic, and I respect the right of anyone to design her own death. As an artist, I particularly could enjoy seeing people treat their deaths as creatively as their lives. I ask only that no one wanting to end her life be forced to live against her will and that she be given the option of exiting with a reliable means made readily available by society; and that an exiting person conscientiously aim to cause no jeopardy to another person's life. If for some internal reason a person would like to end life with a high dive, let her plan carefully not to land on another person. And let her know she has the alternative of an Exit Pill.

What about bizarre means of self-termination? I feel that within the limits of preventing life jeopardy to others, such must be accepted as well as sometimes regretted. If we are to intervene, it must be, I believe, on the side of preventing pathology. But once pathology has invaded a person's being, I don't believe her rights to suicide can justifiably be taken away. We may have to devise temporary holding positions for assessment of one situation or another and for making known the possibility of alternatives. But after that, I don't see as justifiable the forcing of a person to live just because she would resort to some bizarre means of suicide. If a person wants to end life by acting out a bizarre fantasy which will not jeopardize the life of another, why not?

Once a concept emerges in society, there is no way to make it vanish. It may or may not be used and developed, but it cannot be made to go away. And each of us somehow always involved in all decisions. We may or may not like the concept of having the option to abort human fetuses, but the option cannot be made to vanish. One may feel indifferent to the option's existence, but at some level she votes for or against its use all the time. The option of suicide has existed from the beginning of human life, although it is doubtful that it was conceptualized at the outset. It evolved somewhere along the way and is here to stay. The concept of suicide as a human *right* is only now emerging, but it has been born and it, too, is here to stay. It may be fought over and it may be difficult to clarify it and develop the protections essential to any human right. But, I have no doubt, the right of suicide is being clarified and will soon be secure.

Why now? Why after all the ages of human existence with the option of suicide are we suddenly confronted with suicide as a right? Clearly this is a consequence of the marriage in our time of medicine and technology, which, in turn, has given birth to the ineradicable concept of prevention of death, therefore of life forced upon one regardless of one's will. We are already under way in the process of not allowing people to die. Not so-called natural deaths. Or timely deaths. Or wanted deaths. And so, we must, as quickly and effectively as possible, establish that each of us indeed does have a basic right to die at a time and by a means of our choosing. We must have the right to disallow others to press unwanted life upon us. We must have the right to assign responsibility to others to carry out our life endings if we become unable.

It will not be easy for society to come quickly to grips with this, for we are composed of individuals who have passively accepted our life spans being doubled in this century. If we happened to be at a relatively comfortable place on the human spectrum, we have cheered our good luck and been very disinclined to hear the plaintive pleas of those whose disadvantaged lives were worsened by increased longevity. Further, we relatively comfortable people have led the supporting of those systems which work to extend life still further. It is not unusual to be greedy for life when we are comfortable. But note! Many of us who were relatively comfortable a short time ago are getting less and less comfortable and our longer lives are becoming burdensome. We are being confronted with the real—however hidden—costs of life extension. The costs of creating and supporting new institutions—nursing homes, hospices, etc.—and an ever-growing population which cannot make good use of the basic original life span of forty years, to say nothing of a doubled life span. And now we are being born out of the womb of science fiction into a real world of having our bodies and our body parts belonging not to ourselves but to others.

We have blinded ourselves to the reality of our mortality, and so to the most meaningfully rich possibilities of our living. By aiming for extended life we have lost sight of living fully the mortal life at hand. We have given over some of our best resources to creating an illusion of being deathless. Now we may fade in old age into a nursing home or in youth be mangled on the highway and still not die. Our bodies can be plugged into the wall—fuel willing—and be kept functioning mechanically and given replacements of body parts. Isn't it marvelous to have defeated death! To know we can now have "life" guaranteed for as much as a century. And if we can do that, why not two centuries? Forever?

Confidence? Not as total as I'd like. But I believe there is a very high probability that my plan will be effective. Still, when I reach for absolute certainty I do sense a margin of uncertainty. Somewhere I've read that every known method of suicide has been known to fail. What could go wrong with my plan?

Does Seconal have a limited shelf life? During the last months of my illness my body weight has swollen, ought I take a larger dosage? Need I be concerned about the temperature of the drug's storage? I haven't time to ferret out more information. If there had been more time I'd have liked to learn whether my 4500 mg of Seconal might have been compressed into a fewer number of capsules. I did query whether they might be mixed into, say, a milkshake, and was advised against that on the grounds that irritation of membranes en route to the stomach might occur and cause vomiting.

It seems to me that one ought to be able to ask all such questions of any M.D. and expect the doctor to have or to obtain a reliable answer. I have a better than average access to a large number of doctors and have been posing suicide-related questions for years. Generally I've found doctors uninformed. I also gained the impression that they felt as uneasy or even as unable as I to obtain information. I'm sorry I didn't think to employ a medical researcher to work with me on clarifying questions and seeking answers.

It is the marriage of medicine and technology which has thrown into a cocked hat the perception of death which has served us so well through the centuries. We hold people plugged into the wall while we argue about brain waves and whether a mechanically breathing body sans consciousness is alive. We no longer know what death is. We leave it to the experts to argue and come to a decision. I feel profound compassion for the enormity of their undertaking. And I would like to be able to consult our experts. But, thank you, I'd like to decide for myself whether I want my life saved or extended. I want to appoint persons who I feel most share or understand my perceptions to act in my behalf if I become unable. If the experts can create extension of human life spans to one hundred years or more I'd give them my bravos! If they take unto themselves the right to impose upon me— or you—a life whose quality is not satisfactory to the body's resident, then I protest with all my might. I find ominous any force which has the power to impose its will on me.

When my advanced suicide date became known, several doctors became more ready to help my planning even though simultaneously their concern for their own legal liability understandably had to be raised. My own awareness of their potential legal jeopardy proved to be a restraint on my asking for help at this time. This added confirmation to my still too weakly stated view of the importance of planning and obtaining one's means as far before need as possible. When fire breaks out is not the best time to look for an exit. Better that the exit be planned and noted in advance.

I am very moved that several doctors who knew of my advanced suicide date volunteered assistance to my family in the event my effort went awry. That is, that they would go so far as to give me an injection to supplement my own effort. I particularly appreciate their perceptiveness in making their offers to my family rather than to me, for this tells me both their acceptance of my view and their appreciation that the effectiveness of my suicide is as important to my survivors as to me. It touches me deeply that they would risk jeopardy to themselves by extending help to us. We have declined all offers of these several doctors, and also of two nurses, to directly administer any part of my suicide. We would rather suffer the grim risk of an aborted suicide and its sequel than have any part of jeopardy to another. Still, those offers are intensely moving and, hopefully, will serve as building blocks in Exit House's foundation.

It is important to note that all offers of assistance to my family came from professionals who were in a position to have confidence in our dedication to developing the rational suicide concept and understood that there would be no attempt to conceal my suicide. Rather the reverse. Thus, I take it that they were responding to the issues rather than just personally out of affection for any of us.

In my talks with a large sample of doctors I was impressed, sometimes informed, that many doctors would not be hesitant, using caution, to administer willfully a lethal drug to persons with whom they were close if those people wished it and were terminally ill. They felt this to be a fairly common and very concealed practice because a fraction of the medical and nonmedical world would be intensely opposed and litigious. No one I talked with indicated any inclination to get involved in changing these circumstances. This means that untold numbers of persons who would wish to end or have their lives ended would be deprived of the opportunity simply because they lacked a close relationship with an obliging doctor. In this day of increased absence of personal relationship with doctors, it seems, therefore, that laypersons have less chance than ever of obtaining suicide information or other assistance from their doctors.

Another impression worth noting is that a sizable number of doctors volunteered to sign my death certificate in such a manner as to conceal my death's being a suicide. While I'm not at all interested in concealment, I find the ready availability of concealment as confirmation—hardly needed—that suicide statistics are highly unreliable, especially among the population whose economic level might assure personal closeness to a physician. I've heard so often the view that it is easy to commit suicide. Some have said there's no need to develop special means because anyone who wants to end her life can easily do so. What a grossly mistaken notion!

We need to recognize that certainly not all persons looking for a means of ending their lives are at all interested in killing. Perhaps most people who would wish for the ideal sort of Exit Pill yet to be developed—the swift, painless, irreversible type—are not at all interested in killing. *The wish to leave life is profoundly different from the wish to destroy it.* Alas, the only word we have to cover both ends of the spectrum is *suicide*. But surely we can learn to distinguish one end from the other, and then to find ways to come to grips with the less clear in-betweens.

A person at the killing/destructive/angry/maiming/punishing/low self-esteem/impulsive end of the spectrum may find it relatively easy to commit suicide. Maybe. Perhaps such people don't mind making a mess of themselves. Conceivably it excites them to think of blowing out their brains, slashing themselves, jumping in front of a train, etc. If so, perhaps their means of exit is indeed readily accessible. But how different are these suffering humans from those at the other end of the spectrum, who have high self-esteem and no pleasure in killing, but rather—even simply—are coming to a time when they will have spent themselves to such a degree that they feel it appropriate and desirable for them to bring their lives to an end. Self-destructiveness is absent or irrelevant among these people. Their circumstances may be such that ending their lives is indeed a way to protect themselves from some destructive experience such as terminal illness or deteriorating old age.

The attitude that suicide must inherently be expressive of murderous self-destructiveness and lack of self-esteem has seemed absurd and offensive to me as far back as I can remember. When I attempted suicide at age twenty-nine, it is true that my self-esteem was sometimes low. Equally true that usually it was good to excellent. It is true that I was not free of unresolved anger toward my own limitations and those of people whose lives affected mine. But it was my weariness from the burden of struggling with that load which brought me to willingness to relinquish life. I was never interested in killing or hurting myself. With all my longings then for release from life's struggle, I never thought to hurt myself. The notion of self-murder was abhorrent and entirely distinguishable from my longing for relief.

Now that I am about to end my life and still enjoy as much self-esteem and zest for life as anyone I know, I find simply excruciating the notion of suicide being regarded inherently as an expression of bizarre self-murder.

I'm gifted with extraordinarily good resources and strength to rise above this terrible social denial of—violation of—my right to die my rational way. I have had the good fortune to have around me people from whom help could be elicited. And so I dare to die my way anyhow. And, in the process, discover there's a large part of our world which would like to have its rights to a decent death with decent means secured. It is difficult to establish availability and reliability of means, and to create a suitable environment. But I see that with determination it can be done. Every time one can make an open statement about the positive aspects of suicide, the sooner its stigma will vanish and the right to suicide will be recognized and supported for all who wish to avail themselves of it. Unless this right is secured—until it is—all but the few of us who are lucky enough to arrange our suicides, concealed or not, must feel restricted to death by accident, illness, or old age.

Suicide is not just a moment. Suicide is a process which ends in self-termination. If I'm inflicting anything upon myself, it is demanding that I share my view with others. Writing, for me, is torment. But my writing, however intertwined with my suicide process, is separate from the process. Whatever the process, I believe it a maturing experience of living. To go through life knowing your life will be most responsible if you create its ending as well as its content is to go through life with heightened awareness and appreciation of your own potential. To go through life planning a responsible ending of your span—what greater maturing life experience can there then be? To know you have a good means of ending is to not waste life fearing a grim closure.

Having written the foregoing draft about means, having felt as settled in my suicide plan as I believe I likely could be, having now more than one hundred people who are aware of my plan; suddenly I discover I have access to a

cyanide pellet. I've spent a sleepless night grappling with
the fact.

I've arrived at this morning feeling I probably will use
the cyanide. I'm also feeling uncharacteristically hurt
and angry that society has automatically, thoughtlessly
condemned me and mine to an ugly note in a suicide of
peace, love, gentleness, and profound consideration. I, a
gentle loving person trying to make of my life meaningful
value for humankind rather than a simple drifting or self-
indulgence, am confronted with a nearly intolerable deprivation at the time I mean to complete my life's canvas
with its final, and perhaps its most creative, stroke.

It may be that the determination I feel welling within me
to defeat the deprivation which threatens reflects yet un-
ripened conclusions more than real strength, and I may
finally set aside the cyanide and stay with my aforementioned plan. Perhaps (as I said before when referring to
the CIA's use of convulsive drugs for the purpose of
bringing about a swift irreversible death) the experts do
know something I don't. What I don't know about cyanide
is, for the time being, extensive. My impressions are based
more on wisps than on solid facts. I will learn more.

For the moment, my dreams of taking leave of my body
through a peaceful sleep and in the special comfort of the
home I love—these dreams lie drenched in tears. Not yet
abandoned, for I see now more than ever that when I think
of relinquishing those dreams, I feel I might be depriving
my dear ones an experience of rare humanity—no matter
how uneasy may be their approach to it. So I still cling to
the Compazine/Seconal scenario.

The cyanide scenario? My uninformed belief at the moment is that death by cyanide is an ugly sight to behold.
That the receiving body becomes instantly convulsed and
blue. It expels the contents of the intestinal tract. I know

instantly that I want no one who cares about me to be left with such a grim final image of me. So I may use the cyanide only if I am willing to create a different final stroke than I intended, if I can bring myself to walk away from my dear ones and my home, if I can take myself to some impersonal place and there leave behind an unnecessarily violated body—the body I have no wish to make ugly.

If I am to pursue such a course, then I must devise some system by which my body will be found quickly and un-mysteriously so that my circle need not be hung on tenter-hooks as to whether I have carried out my mission all right. I must arrange for my body to be identified by someone peripheral or beyond the intimate circle. I feel forced against my will into plotting as though I were staging a crime. Rage boils at the social insult. Personally I care not at all that the medical examiners will see my uglied re-mains and be compelled to commit other violations upon them in order to investigate—at considerable taxpayer cost—the cause of death, which I would gladly have registered with them. I, my consciousness, will be gone from those remains and will not feel the probings nor the fires of cremation. Let them do what they must. Let them also know that their investigation would have no purpose if society didn't force the indignity of concealment upon its members.

I'm surprised at how often my reflections bring me back to my intimate survivors and the sense of their being de-prived by the cyanide scenario. I think of the—of our—clinging as I step away from them and from my home. My body still held erect by my personhood. Then—how many days later?—they receive into their hands my body's ashes, ready for recycling. All right. Not a grotesquerie. But is there, indeed, not something taken from their ex-perience?

I think of each of them and know it might have been their death I'd have to accept. True, I would not need to experience their dying. And yet, I think how, if any of them would be dying, our separation would somehow feel more whole or more "right"—what word do I want?—if I could hold them lovingly in my arms through their final breaths. No less pain in such a separating, but such a very different and somehow healing pain.

So I tell myself, don't take the cyanide. Don't deprive your circle of the possibility of comforting/loving each other into and through my last breaths. But then I imagine those remote possibilities of my Seconal scenario aborting. And I can't let go of the pellet. But now—quite apart from my loved ones—could I take that ugly convulsive step in my solitude? Would I not become frozen in absolute terror? If only I could redirect the energy of the intense anger I feel, transforming it into another sort of strength! Could I do that? I feel drawn to the challenge and excited to think I might find in myself strength to defeat defeat.

It is evening now. It seems almost like fate that I had a consult scheduled for today. I've been scheduling meetings with various doctors specifically to inform them of my plan and to say that I would appreciate it if they would tell me if they know of any way to make it more swift, or more irreversible. I never ask or press doctors for information. No doctor, after hearing me out, has declined to give me an opinion, and gradually my plan has been refined by these consultations. Interestingly, no one has submitted a bill. No one has seemed shocked. All have indicated or stated they would end their lives rather than undergo terminal cancer. But all have been inclined to think they would not exit as early as I. When they ask about this and I tell them my feelings, they all seem respectful of my choice.

In today's consultation I informed the doctor that I now have access to a cyanide pellet. There was no occasion to reveal my emotional mulling of its possible use. The doctor immediately discouraged my use of the cyanide on the grounds of its being so unpleasant. Further and more important, the doctor detailed for me the impossibility of reversal once there is no pulse and no breathing and the eyes are dilated. The time it takes to be thus dead varies from one body to another. Twenty minutes was confirmed as probable time for sleep and then a coma to set in. The coma would probably last three hours before death.

It was also suggested that I take as many more than 4500 mg as I can. It was wondered whether I had ever taken Seconal before and was, therefore, familiar with the woozy feeling that develops as the pills take effect, and whether I might feel frightened when that occurred, since I would know that death was coming. I'm familiar with that woozy feeling of Seconal and don't consider it even slightly unpleasant. Rather, I find it a welcome feeling when it is invited. When I'm ready to exit I will most certainly welcome it, and I am not at all concerned about any last moment distress.

While I feel more at ease that the Seconal exit will not abort and will be effective, and at the same time am relieved not to feel I must consider a cyanide exit, I must say I'm ever so grateful to have had the opportunity of experiencing the facing of the alternative. I'm enormously grateful to the person who had the courage to volunteer making the cyanide available. However, I'm reminded again of the unfairness of being privileged. Think of the vast majority of people who have no medical friends to turn to for forthright counsel and supplies.

Rights and Assistants (Medical, Practical, Protective, Personal, Legal)

It is sometime in the future. You have the will to bring your life to an end and, from your own point of view, good reason. By luck you've learned of painless, reasonably swift, and probably irreversible means to stop your body's breathing. Somehow, you've managed to acquire the means. You anticipate that you will have no physical or emotional difficulty ingesting the sedative, that you will easily drift into a gentle sleep and then out of consciousness and life within the next half-hour. You feel at peace with your readiness to relinquish a portion of life in order to die well; happy that you do not demand of yourself that you live on into a time whose quality you believe will be below your standards. Now what?

You may not be elderly or terminally ill, but chances are that you are either or both. Chances are also that no matter how resolved you are, no matter how tenderly you hold those red capsules in your palm, your hand will be frozen short of your mouth. The outside world—if they knew—would be inclined to claim that *not* taking the capsules reflects your instinctual attachment to life; that your life instinct is greater than your death instinct. I, however—

trusting you have arrived at your readiness with deepest thoughtfulness—would jump to no such conclusion. I respect your right to design your life span all the way. I'm ready to believe you've resolved any relevant ambivalence about accepting your life's end. Those who insist your hesitancy reflects unwillingness on your part are, I daresay, projecting their own reluctance to come to grips with their own dying. Perhaps they are relishing your hesitancy and reading it as confirmation that there is no good reason for them to regard their own finiteness.

Whatever the base of their common reaction, a more useful understanding of your hesitation can be found, I believe, in your own mind. Imagine yourself now being ready, willing, and able but with your hand stayed. What is in your mind at this moment? Is your fear one of death or is it one of life following some abortion of your plan? It is conceivable that, as fully as you've researched your means of dying, as confident as you are of its effectiveness, and as carefully as you've placed yourself against premature discovery and consequent forced revival, some utterly unpredictable event might interfere. You've planned meticulously so there will be no disruption. There will be no telltale delivery of newspapers at your door. You've arranged for your building superintendent to accept special deliveries "during my absence." But you can't arrange that some building emergency—a broken pipe, a fire—will not cause the police to break into your house thirty seconds after you swallow the last capsule. Unbelievable things do disrupt acts of suicide. Who'd have believed that a man jumped from a high ledge of one of New York City's skyscrapers and was blown by a wind gust back into the building through a window a few floors below? Many a victim of such incredible sagas has been forced to live an unwanted maimed life.

As you've mulled your present plan into shape you've experienced both resentment over having to resort to stealth and amusement over finding yourself engaged in plotting as though you were a common criminal. If only the world would understand how sensible your decision is and relieve you of the absurd secrecy! You realize, as you work in the dark, that there have been untold thousands—millions?—of people who have struggled alone to find a reasonable way to end their lives. How utterly cruel that they have been deprived of social assistance! How deeply you long for assistance. But where can you turn?

Look again into your own mind while you stare at those bright capsules. Who do you see? Who is it you most wish would help you? Is it not the very people whose images come into your mind as you raise your hand? Isn't it their facial expressions as they are confronted with your suicide which floods your imagination and stays your hand? They are as frozen into those terrible images as your hand is frozen in front of you. The silence roars unbearably full of the unuttered gasps of horror, grieved sobbing, and the electric hum of gossip based upon invented explanations barely, if at all, related to your reality. Those faces tell shock, disbelief, injury, dismay, bewilderment. All, you know, unnecessary. If you were acting out some irrational need, perhaps those images would please you. But your suicide intent is *rational*. You have neither wish nor need to inflict such pain. It is *their* reading of your act which pains them. It is *their* refusal to hear you which spreads guilt across their faces. No matter how deeply you know that it is your right and reasonable time to die, you also know they will use your suicide as a trigger for their own devastating emotions. And oh how it hurts that those special people will think less of you; how horrible that they might turn angrily against you for experiencing what they regard as their failure to make a longer life of desirable quality for you. You are, indeed, trapped between two grim alternatives. You can end your life knowing your act will be used to trigger a mushroom cloud of ugliness— large or small—no matter what your intent. Or you can abandon your sensible suicide plan and head into an indefinitely long unwanted lifetime. If you weren't at all depressed before, now—while facing such paralyzing alternatives—you have solid reason to feel gloom.

The faces in your imagination haunt you with their emotion. You would speak such comforting words to them, if only they would listen. But they are deaf. Deaf! Okay, you vacillate, you'll stay and endure life in order to spare them their anguish. How bad could it be? In your mind you hear a babble of voices. There are mouths uttering conflicting declarations. "Life is eternal. Beyond earthly death there is life eternal with opportunity to reach ever more glorious states." Simultaneously, "Rail against earthly death. Regardless of life quality, extend bodily life ever longer. End death." There are words coming from people who wouldn't dream of taking another's life because to do so would be tantamount to playing God. Yet they have no twinge of conscience over forcing others to live unwanted lives. And that, too, is playing God.

Words flow to tell you life is beautiful, to be clung to at all costs regardless of pain to you and yours and/or diminished resources and/or your personal sense of having had enough of it. You are told you are a coward to want no more. A coward! A bad influence. Evil. A quitter. No labels of strength, wisdom, compassion for you! You must be deranged to want out of life. Deranged. Depressed. That's it! Your mental outlook has become disordered. You really shouldn't feel bothered that you can no longer care for yourself in your own home, or don't care to do so.

So you tell yourself you will live on. No matter how little taste you can muster for the task. Maybe you'll be lucky and get turned on to life.

You try to lower your hand. Anything to stop the imagined harangue of those encircling faces. Anything! Even living! But your hand will not budge. A scrapbook bulging with newspaper clippings and magazine articles and scribbled notes of things you've heard with increasing frequency in recent years comes into your mind's eye, displacing the babbling faces of those who find you disturbing.

The pages turn. You read of all the things society does for people whose financial resources run dry because of the increased cost of living, the impossibility of saving, decreased employability, greater need for specialized education and its increased unavailability, the rapidly changing marketplace which overnight makes your hard-won skills obsolete. But you chide yourself out of permitting such a disheartening thought. Surely you'll find some way to keep your home. Even if you no longer have the energy and means to do so.

Well, if worst comes to worst, society will liquidate your belongings and generously provide you with free quarters. True, you might not like the place, but so what? You'd have the marvelous satisfaction of being alive! Even if you have to move onto a welfare allowance and into different quarters in a different neighborhood, away from the people and life style which have been yours. Surely as long as you are alive you'll be able to make friends among your new neighbors. Take heart.

Your body showing signs of wear? You've had touches of arthritis for years and now it seems more bothersome? Well, some pages hold promise of a cure for arthritis. Government pamphlets—generously free—indicate that if your arthritis progresses far enough doctors could give you whole new joints. Now that's good news! No need to fret about arthritis in your future. And if you get cancer or heart disease, there are pages which tell of marvels coming or already available. No matter what misfortunes might befall you, there *can* be no rational reason to bow out of the great goodness of life.

With all the marvelous new technology at hand, there's a whole new burgeoning industry providing livelihood for thousands of people and bolstering our economy, all to whet your appetite for life with assurance that the industry is engaged in an all-out high-cost battle to develop life extension and supports for your body. Assurance that your body can be kept alive for a hundred years is quite at hand. One hundred and fifty years is just around the corner. Isn't that what everyone wants? You too! Feel your life instinct driving you on! You don't? Well now, that's very limited and unsporting of you! Would you have the market glutted with all the new services and no one to use them? Would you deprive someone who needs to work to support a family or a life style the benefit of creating and maintaining services to keep you alive? You would? You are that inconsiderate?

Hold your hand in catatonic limbo just a little longer and we won't have to worry about your impudent "irreverence for life." Give us just a little longer, relinquish just a little more command of your own life and then we can move along. We'll give you tranquilizers—free, if your purse has grown empty—so you won't have to fret any longer. We'll move you into one of our very nice, very clean nursing homes. See how lovely the lobby is? Polished, neat, flowered. Friendly staff. You'll love your new life. No more house cleaning or shopping or cooking or worrying about the rent. Just settle back and do as you're told, and you can watch TV in the group room or attend the special events designed to keep you happy—singalongs, dancing, entertainment, crafts. Yes, you'll love it if you just co-operate. And yes, it's true that if you insist on fretting, even after the tranquilizers, we'll have to move you away from the more public areas. It wouldn't be fair to people who want to live as long as possible to have to listen to complaining all the time. Besides, complainers require a different kind of staff and drug than do the noncom-plainers. You surely understand that, don't you?

More pages turn. A large section on Karen Ann Quinlan. A vegetable for years. And every page reminds you be-tween the lines of how in your own lifetime people have stopped dying at home. When dying seems imminent—whether people are at home or in a nursing home—it has become essential to ship them to a hospital. That is what you do for your dying relatives or friends out of your love of them. To keep them at home means earlier death, which of course reflects your lack of affection. If someone you love is dying, the way to demonstrate your love is to hospitalize the person and document that you will pay whatever the costs to keep the body alive as long as pos-sible. If the body's resident pleads for death, ignore the plea. It must be a mere impulse of a mind disturbed by the threat of death. If you can keep the body alive, maybe a cure will result and then the body's resident will be thrilled at your devotion. And so happy to be alive that there'll be no concern about getting the bills paid.

There really are people who dream of life eternal within their earthly bodies. People so averse to death that they channel their funds into freezing their bodies so that they may be revived eventually. We have vertical cemeteries now and untold numbers of human bodies mechanically existing. Soon high-rise buildings of living mummies.

Daddies and kids, too. And, naturally, pets. And why not favorite floral arrangements?

Are you recoiling from these very real directions? Are you relinquishing yourself—or at least your body—to the manager of these directions? Or are you going to take command of your life?

You find yourself exasperated by your dilemma. You know you are reasonable and must have the right to end your life. You know "they" cannot reasonably have the right to force you to live. But while our social mores stand, you have no choice but to subject yourself to an unwanted existence, or to subject those you care about to suffer their reactions to your suicide. But wait! Is there not a heretofore unnoticed alternative?

How about eliciting the assistance of those you care about? Don't you suppose that somewhere in their hearts— however barricaded from ready access—they truly would rather not be caught up in forcing unwanted existence upon you? And would not want such imposed upon themselves? Pondering such an alternative, for the first time, your arm relaxes enough to let your hand rest. You feel that a window has opened and hope for reason sweetens the air. You drift into a wonderful dream. In the dream you see you have come to a readiness to draw your life to a close. Your closest family and friends gather into a circle around you as you speak with them. It is all rather simple. Almost as though you had all been attending a large party and you've just drawn your circle around you to tell them that you've had enough of the party and would like to leave. You appreciate that it is a good party and that some of the best parts of it are yet to come. Even so, you've had as much as you want for yourself. You feel ready to leave. You don't want to disrupt the party. You want your circle to resume its participation. You've called them together simply because you don't want to leave without a good-bye embrace. You don't want them to be startled or baffled by your absence. You want them to know you are all right. And happy for them to continue on.

No one questions your right to leave. Your wish is readily respected. People say lovely things to you. They tell you your presence will be missed—however much accepted. They share with you the wish not to disrupt the party. So they *offer* to facilitate your departure. They say they will take responsibility for conveying to others your reason for leaving; clarifying that your departure simply expressed that you no longer felt sufficient desire or energy for partying; clarifying—if need be—that your absence was not meant to express a negative view of the party, but, rather, a positive need to withdraw from it in order to attend to personal matters. They ask you to please tell them anything else they might do to ease your departure. They want to assist you. You tell them that you love them and that the best thing they can do now to facilitate your exit is to resume partying for their sake and so that you need not feel your exit as a disruption. The dream ends with everyone walking you to the door. There you all embrace with deep loving respect for one another. Yes, it is a lovely dream. And a telling one.

You resolve that you will begin immediately to discuss openly with others the possibility of creatively using rational suicide as a means of closing one's life. From the outset you realize that if you can elicit discussion and interest, there probably would evolve in your own social world a number of people ready to assist one another. Also that such a small group might gradually expand through society at large in such a way that assistance now needed would eventually become unnecessary.

You don't suppose the need for assistants could disappear

overnight. You realize that human rights never emerge without evolving through phases of protest, overreactions, abuses, and misunderstandings. But now that you are on to recognizing that there must be vast numbers of people around the globe who are coming to a time of awareness of suicide's positive potential, you feel a confidence that assistance must be close at hand, ready to emerge. Perhaps—dare we imagine!—in time to be of use to you, yourself!

Now you look at your red capsules and—if you've time—you set them aside. You also set aside the question of whether to live longer and risk being trapped in unwanted existence, or commit suicide and risk your circle's tormenting itself and sullying your name. You give yourself two tasks. One, to raise your circle's consciousness of the issues. Two, to clarify just what assistance is needed. The second question seems the easier, more immediate probably. Achieving its answer will complete the first task.

Well, to start, you certainly want medical assistance. You've ferreted out that 4500 mg of Seconal that will bring your life to a gentle end. You have confidence in that information. Even so, you wish you had medical assistants who could provide you with solid answers—not guesses—about your means to a rational suicide. Could your capsules' shelf life or temperature of storage have diminished their strength? Given your body weight, need you take so much? You suspect that your medical advisers directed you to the amounts you plan by relying more on generalizations than specifics. Might your Seconal be made ingestible in a form other than forty-five capsules? Your medical advisers discouraged you from spilling the capsules' content into, say, a milkshake, and said an injection would be more efficient. But you feel you cannot inject yourself and do not want anyone else to have the responsibility of ending your life, particularly while such assistance may be subject to prosecution. Still, you wonder, might not the Seconal be compressed into fewer capsules or a tablet?

But that's not all the assistance you want in reference to means. You'd like someone to assist you by researching the experts who have specifically addressed the issue of developing an instant, painless, irreversible means of death. What were their findings? How do these findings compare with means more commonly used? Is cyanide—allegedly the means recommended by experts, and generally unavailable—as painless as the fairly available Seconal? Even though the former allegedly brings death in a convulsion? Is there an alternative as comfortable as Seconal which is or can be made irreversible? Might an assistant locate a qualified source, able and willing, to document answers to such questions?

Yes, a *medical assistant* would be a treasure. But your confidence in the Seconal means you have at hand is such that you personally are feeling less pressed for means assistance than for other assistance. You'd like to have a *practical assistant*. Someone (or more than just one) to help you think through and carry out the practical issues of closing your life. You'd very much like to organize your affairs so that no one will be stuck with the burden of cleaning up after you. You also want someone to distribute your possessions as you wish rather than leave them to be scrambled over or abandoned and wasted because survivors feel restrained from taking what they want for fear of appearing greedy. Your will might need refinement. Your insurance may need to be reviewed, especially any recently purchased insurance. Most insurance benefits will not be restricted by your suicide, but some would be and you want that clarified.

Having reached your suicide decision by choice rather than desperation, such practical settlement of your affairs need not be difficult. Quite the contrary. It is a pleasure to have the opportunity to review and order your affairs. It can provide you with an extraordinarily rich, beautiful, sentimental final phase of life. (I can vouch for that!) Practical assistance for such closing tasks can be drawn from many directions—sheer muscle power for moving and cleaning, accountants and lawyers for business counsel, etc. Obviously, such assistance would be vastly enhanced if it was drawn from people with whom you could be open about your suicide and who would respect your decision.

Having even one person in whom you can confide and whom you can trust to protect your suicide from interruption would be—in this day and age—of exceptional value. There are numerous and difficult issues to consider, however, even if you feel you have someone you might ask to become your *protective assistant.*

Conceivably, you could set up a protective assistant who would not know that it is your suicide being protected. You could hire a professional to guard your door against entrance for a prescribed period of time, but such a guard would be of little help if that unexpected event occurred— a fire or broken plumbing line—thirty seconds after you're snugly into your suicide sleep. Being as much a victim of our antisuicide mores as others commonly are, the professional, discovering you unconscious, probably would take the lead in hospitalizing you, thus causing your stomach to be pumped and your body to be resuscitated into an unwanted state of existence. No, your protector had better know what is being protected.

All right. You take a friend into your confidence. He or she is sympathetic and wants to stand guard. If the interfering event is the plumbing line, your friend can simply close your bedroom door and steer servicepeople away from discovering your dying. If the event is fire, well, whatever flash judgment occurs will prevail. But at least your friend's knowledge of your wish will significantly improve the chance of your suicide's success. Or will it?

Have you thought to prepare your friend not to be distressed if your dying body makes movements or sounds, as dying bodies do? Have you considered the depth of your friend's sympathy for your action? Is your friend so stable that society's intense indoctrination to rescue a dying person will not be triggered automatically by your dying? Is your friend's acceptance of your suicide truly resolved? And what about your friend's feeling about assisting you? Morally resolved, your friend might well still be suffering fear of legal jeopardy. What can you do to alleviate that? Or your friend's feelings about how others would regard his or her assistance?

Thanks to a brilliant idea on the part of Doris Portwood, author of *Common Sense Suicide* (Dodd, Mead & Co., 1978), you might have protective assistance available to you sooner than you expect through a reliable, responsible service. It was her idea to form, within communities, groups of people who respect one's right to commit suicide and are willing to provide protective services. Such groups probably would be composed of people who accept that they are approaching the end of their lives and would like such protective service available for themselves as well as others. As a group they would consider what issues need attention, what to expect, and how to help each other while providing service. Of course, there would need to be some commitment within the group to stand by one another in the event their service was challenged along the way. These assistants could keep each other company while sitting. It would be nice having each other to share discussions and questions; to talk out indoctrinated impulses to "rescue" someone who doesn't want to be "rescued"; to reassure each other that a body sound they hear is not a cry for help but, rather, simply the sound of the body's relaxing muscles and consequent expulsion of air from the lungs or of bowel and bladder content. They could have prepared themselves in conference with the exiting person with a plan of action in the event of spontaneous abortion of the suicide act, i.e., what to do if the body regurgitates the sedative. This is highly unlikely if the exiter prepares properly. However, an exiter might want assistants to know her or his wishes in such an unlikely event.

Organized groups of protective assistants probably would be able to avail themselves from among their membership of medical information which would help them know when the exiter is dead beyond resuscitation. At such a point they would end their service by placing whatever call the exiter had planned to start the process of body disposition. That process would ideally have been prearranged with practical assistants.

For anyone wanting to commit suicide, there could be no advantage more comforting than to have *personal assistants*—even a few relatives or friends who so respect the exiter's wish to bring her or his own life span to an end that they would—as in the dream of leaving the party—turn to you asking what they could do to facilitate and ease your suicide. Wouldn't you love to know that, whenever you are ready to die, there will be family and friends who will reach out to help you die at the time and in the manner of your choice; to say they respect your right and to ask what they can do to help you? To have developed such assistance in your life must reflect your having lived well. Absence of such a circle would not, conversely, necessarily reflect a poorly lived life. For the time being it must reflect social blindness to the need. However, even in this time of blindness, we can begin to bring about the changes which will lead to awareness; to a time when if one hasn't understanding and supportive friends and relatives, there will be understanding and support provided by the larger social system, available to those who wish such service. Of course, no one need ever be required to end her, his, or another's life.

For those who would consider the possibility of developing a circle for themselves, I'd like to tell something of my own experience. I'm not suggesting that mine be repeated. It cannot be. But there are guidelines and suggestions to be drawn from it.

First of all, I would recommend the earliest possible start to find people with whom you can discuss suicide as a rational life-planning potential. Of course, you can expect to find people with closed or opposing minds whom you won't be able to engage. Chances are you can expect to find surprises. You'll find greater openness to general discussion of people being kept alive in nursing homes for decades, of lives being extended even when there can be no substantial hope for a qualitatively good life. Death and dying are increasingly entering the realm of day-to-day conversation. Suicide usually is separated out from the discussion, however.

Discussions on death and dying generally are related to terminally ill or very aged people and not thought of in terms of life planning. The mention of suicide generally casts a pall. Programmed images of madness and failure and ugliness leap into the mind. However, when there are general discussions of death and dying, listen. Watch for discussants whose minds seem open. Watch for an opportunity to raise questions. Ask whether anyone thinks we might find a way to manage our lives so we don't have to go through life fearing an extended period of dying—even though it is possible now for one to be so drugged through extended life that one need not suffer physical pain. Find a time to raise questions about society's right to impose extended life on persons who don't want it. There are endless numbers of questions you can raise with others which you and they will find interesting to discuss. And if you keep in mind that you are on the alert to find persons whose interests are such that they could also discuss suicide with you, then I'm confident you're in for a surprising find. If *you* are interested, you will find others interested too.

At first in these explorations it may seem necessary to keep discussion very generalized. Any move to personalize discussion to the lives of discussants may trigger a guardedness which interferes. We're so programmed to believe it is bad to openly consider suicide that some energy has to be invested to cross the line. Stay alert in conversations. Assuming, now, that your considerations are rational, I'd urge you to realize that the sooner you can venture with someone to open up your own rational considerations, the sooner your own circle of mutual assistance will begin taking shape. Your only real risk is that someone whom you've regarded as having an open mind will prove to be less open than you imagined and will back off from your effort, wondering if you're getting depressed. So you can bear that, can't you? And don't be surprised if your skeptic comes back to explore your thinking. In the interim, try someone else.

How about venturing in some generalized discussion to volunteer that you personally can imagine situations in which you'd feel good about yourself if you would find a way to help another person end her or his life at a chosen time? Thus, coming around to your point in a direct but possibly less alarming way. How about saying, outright, that you find merit in the potential of rational suicide, and opening a discussion of its paradoxical life enrichment?

However you approach your social exploration, if you stay alert and increasingly sharpen your own understanding and beliefs, you'll find yourself developing a sort of mutual aid society whose participants can turn to one another for deeper appreciation as well as assistance. With a little luck and effort, you can help each other gather into your circle each sort of assistant any of you might need—medical, protective, practical, or personal. The sooner you start gathering and participating in a suicide-assistant circle, the more effective that circle can be if ever you elect to call upon it for yourself.

Certainly, for the time being it must be easier for any such assistant circle to provide help when there is no pressure upon it for immediate performance. Pressure for immediate assistance may be entirely rational or an expression of madness. It may be that either should be assisted, but certainly each differently. And in the early days of exploratory experimental circles which have little guiding precedent, it has to be advantageous for a circle's considerations to have as few time demands as possible. I'd hate to see any circle rule out assistance to someone who wanted it immediately, for there must be many good reasons for it to be given. But anticipating that assistant circles will evolve, I'd like to see them taking their time to evolve most thoughtfully.

It was possible for me to develop my own circle rather quickly because of the happenstance of precancer explorations and alertness for persons open to sharing exploration. However, as far as developing the best-quality circle is concerned, I think it would be better if my circle had formed earlier, and was not focused at the outset upon the particular need of a single person (me). Because of the time frame I set for myself, my circle came into being with givens which were peculiar to my circumstances, and so drew into it persons who might otherwise have been disinclined to participate. Still, perhaps it is my experiencing the earnestness of participation of those who'd rather not have found themselves in such an assistant circle which enables me to see that even among the *resistant* population there is valuable assistance to be tapped. Further, it is my impression that among the resistant assistants there are people who—as they open themselves to the task—provide some of the best-thought-through help.

A word of caution as you set out to form a suicide-assistant circle: Those people who most openly and readily declare that they support the right sometimes are the least able to bring their own lives to an end. My impression is that their intention is honest enough, but that, lacking the experience of talking out the practical and emotional issues of committing suicide, they simply are ill equipped, practically and emotionally, to act upon their intent when the time comes when they might wish they could have acted.

I've known numerous people who have readily declared agreement with my stance and insisted that they would absolutely end their lives before the onset of senility, before the onset of a terminal phase of illness. These same people either have not had the opportunity for discussing their intent with anyone—including me—or else they have avoided it. Several of the people to whom I refer did just that when I—anticipating the obstacles which were ahead of them—tried to open discussion. Most of these people were elderly, and from their plights I have learned the urgency of developing a pro-suicide belief system long, long before you might be ready to avail yourself of it.

If your active interest in rationally ending your life begins in, say, your still perky sixties, chances are the odds are quite against creating a good death for yourself at a time of your choice and in a manner of your choice. Chances are that you will die, instead, of illness or in a state of some degree of debilitation due to your aging process. You'd like to discuss what you're feeling with someone, but who? Like you, your peers are clinging more tenaciously than ever to whatever makes life pleasurable. It's more fun to go to a concert than to discuss life endings. At best you can get a few sentences exchanged about what a pity it is that Aunt Mandy couldn't afford to live in her own home any longer and had to be placed in a nursing home; how the family saw to it that she got the nicest one possible and what a relief it is to know she'll be cared for. The family was worrying about her getting depressed as her funds ran out. Now they can rest in peace knowing that if she gets depressed she can be drugged. They've done all they can to ensure her living as long as possible. That's what the family has been programmed to believe is the most loving thing they can do for her.

Would you like to have gone to Mandy and said, "You know, Auntie, that your life belongs to you. You can live it out to the end if you want to. But you don't have to, I want you to know. If you live it out to the end, given our family history and medicine's life-extending technology, you'll probably live another fifteen years or so. Think you'd like to do that? Knowing you have an alternative to living a decade or more in a nursing home? Suicide used to be thought bad, and I know some of our family might be shocked if you decided you wanted out now. But I wouldn't be. I wouldn't fault you at all. If you want to go into the nursing home, I'll love and help you do that. If you'd rather end your life now, I'll love and help you know how to do that too."

I've known a few Mandys. What I've found is that it is no simple matter to offer assistance even when you want to. If you and Auntie—or Uncle!—have never discussed such matters, and you know she's indoctrinated to think suicide is bad or immoral, or would bring shame upon the family, chances are that you can't open her head to suicide as a respectable action, particularly when she's already in distress at being confronted with the loss of her home. She probably thinks of suicide as a desperate act of madness. She very well might spend much of the rest of her life trying to ward off such notions emerging within herself. She may convince herself she is going mad because she no longer feels zest for living or visiting in the group room or eating or anything. She may withdraw emotionally to contain her distress and her anger at being trapped.

Or perhaps Mandy isn't the type of person who's been particularly religious or insistently traditional. She's been a more outspoken type. Used to laugh and say no one would ever catch her in a nursing home! You wonder why she's meekly, though unhappily, accepting admission. Why? Obviously, she didn't know how to choose an exit date and prepare herself to use it. Why didn't she just "do it" as she kept saying she would? And now, is it too late? Well, that depends more on you than on her. How ready, willing, and able are you to offer help? Your limitations are Mandy's, too.

In my experience there was Helen. She was in her early sixties (I in my fifties and stirring Exit House privately).

I hardly ever saw her when she didn't make some comment about another person being dumb enough to get senile or go into a nursing home. She kept saying she'd cut her throat first. I could imagine her ending her life, but not so bloodily. I wondered whether she really meant her forceful declarations. She made her pronouncements out of proportion to any gloom I could note her experiencing. I supposed she had reflected upon her future and wanted to know a good way out. She was not a person I felt inclined to socialize with. We just happened to have frequent neighborly contact. It was also a time before I had any thought of consciously developing a suicide-assistant circle for myself. (Frankly, it didn't occur to me that that would be a sensible thing for each person to do until I found I had such a circle.) One day I ventured to tell Helen that I was writing about a place where people who wanted to end their lives could do so with assistance. She gave me a broad smile of approval and shared the view I then had that it would be a long time before Exit House could be transformed from fiction into reality. Still, she now understood our shared area of respect for suicide. Once I told her I wished she had a means other than throat cutting. She laughed and assured me she always had enough medicine to put herself into a final sleep. I told her that made me happy for her. There was no need for me to offset my spontaneous statement by uttering a cliché that she should live to a hundred. She understood that my remark was one of affection and not rejection.

As her sixties were running out, I saw Helen battling depression at one point. She began to seem withdrawn. Audaciously, I spoke with her son, who lived at a distance and behaved as though he wanted me to "keep an eye on" Helen. I told him I would, of course, notify him of any significant need Helen had, but I wanted him to know that I thought she was potentially suicidal and I would not consider interfering if I knew her to be making a suicide attempt. He was not a person about to engage in discussion of the matter. Still, I was impressed that he seemed to think it a blessing if Helen died and that he was rather pleased by my stance.

Helen and I never discussed the critical issue of setting a time, although I imagine each of us had thought about the numbering of her days. Helen had a stroke and moved on into her seventies. Even with the luck of freedom from financial woes and the assurance of being able to live in her own home no matter how long she lived, she lived a dreary woebegone life. There came a time when we were geographically separated and our occasional brief contacts were by phone. One night she called and for the umpteenth time said she wished she could just die. Only this time she asked if I knew how much sedation she would need to end her life. She sounded pitiful. I gave her the best information I had garnered. Two weeks later I heard by the grapevine that Helen was dead. Everyone said it was good that she was out of her misery. No one on the line knew how or when she had died. I didn't speak of our conversation. Her son never bothered to notify me, although he knew of our close neighborly relationship across a decade. I don't know how Helen died. But I hope she loved herself enough to put herself to sleep when she'd had enough living.

Ruth was another sort of person. An elegant intellectual. Also about ten years my senior. When she was in her late sixties I sent her a copy of my embryonic manuscript of *Exit House*, asking for her reaction. I very much wanted her criticism. I also very much wanted to open a line of communication between us. It appeared to me she was heading into a really tough old age, one in which a progressive illness would slowly strip her of her ability to use herself as she had developed her abilities. I realized she must know it even better than I. I respected her right not to open discussion of her personal concerns with me, but I cared about her considerably and really wanted to let her know she had, in me, someone who would be open to discussion of suicide if, perchance, that subject held interest for her.

At first I was disappointed in her reaction. Usually she was generous in giving criticism when it was requested, but on *Exit House* she seemed rather stingy, returning the manuscript to me almost coldly. I was slow to appreciate that she had been gripped by the questions with which my work confronted her. I began to realize from her veiled remarks during subsequent contacts that she had initially resented the questions as though I had intruded into her private world. But Ruth made no move to distance herself from me. On the contrary, her invitations increased. Gradually I began to notice that when she would call me she would sometimes open a little talk about my book. Under the guise of objective interest I began to feel she was seeking more assistant-type information from me. I also noticed that she skirted any approach to the subject when anyone else was around—even my husband, whom she knew to be a participant in my thinking.

As of this writing Ruth is alive and significantly crippled by her progressive illness. About three years have passed. Our talks—relevant to the Exit House concept—remain distinctly guarded and absolutely on her terms, except for a few rather aggressive moves on my part. About eighteen months ago I once deliberately brought to the fore discussion of the issues when Mel was present. Ruth responded openly, and she since is given to calling me on occasion to ask me a sharply focused question on the subject. Once, she wanted to know in detail about means. Of course, I shared all my information. And somewhere along the way there were a few very touching exchanges in which she revealed that she had examined all the religio-philosophical issues and had concluded she'd truly like to end her life. Yet her hand was stayed by that circle of familiar faces in her mind. Most especially a child. She couldn't bear the shame and disappointment she imagined her family and friends would feel. Nor could she tolerate her images of those people telling her grandchildren. No, she said, she could not.

Then came the turn of events in my life, and eventually I informed Ruth that I would end my life soon—instead of around 1992, as I had told her. Of course, she had thought I might have second thoughts as 1992 approached. But now she experienced my facing my 1979 suicide. She was particularly eager to learn my family's reaction, and was astonished at their degree of acceptance. Particularly at my son and daughter-in-law's sense of pride in my fortitude and their determination to be open with my grandchildren about my suicide. I, myself, had been taken by surprise, and I suggested to Ruth that our children may have more readiness to be realistic than we give them credit for. Certainly my children appreciated—for their sakes as well as my own—that I would end my life rather than subject us all to terminal cancer. Perhaps if she could open discussions with her children she'd find they could be deeply respectful of her ending her life rather than endure her suffering, which may well go on years longer.

From experience with Helen, Ruth, and others over sixty, at this stage of our culture's development I'm quite pessimistic that rational suicide can be much of a viable alternative. On the other hand, if there would evolve some significant degree of social approval and more people would extend help to the elderly—enabling them to see suicide as a rational alternative and offering to assist them—I've no doubt there are many who would take the alternative. Having spent a lifetime concealing any perception of suicide as rational, it may be too much to expect today's elderly to leap boldly out of the closet. Some who could be helped to close their lives might still need to conceal their act. I gather that this is a quite common practice among those privileged to have relationships with doctors willing to risk faking a death certificate.

What else can I say about assistants? What leaps to my mind is personal. I flash with longing that I could have had assistance available to me without having to develop it myself out of resistant forces. How marvelously different these last months would have been. There were so many things I longed to do other than write this book. How marvelous it would have been if I had grown up in a world where most of us were able to take responsibility for our life's length as well as content; where we had grown to assume that an essential part of our living was to be creating a good death for ourselves on a date of our personal responsible selection; where we would grow into social responsibility for helping one another with the dying part of life as an integral part of living; where we would all appreciate that accident or illness might necessitate a premature dying but that late dying need never be; where dying later than one would wish would be as archaic as having more children than one wishes or can care for reasonably; where we turn our resources fully into wanted life and never into unwanted existence.

Simultaneously, I want to shout with joy that against social odds a circle of assistance has rallied around me. And, as a direct consequence of this assistance being available to me, I feel I have personally discovered a profound phenomenon which one day will be open to all. Namely, that dying need not be awful. Given acceptance, social assistance, pain-relieving technology, and protection against the danger of being forced to live against one's will, it can be a truly good experience. Separation may always inherently risk some discomfort. Many mothers know that childbirth need not always be excruciating. Wanting to separate when it is the right time makes the separation possible, at least, and enhances the chances that mother, child, father, family, and friends will find the beauty of the experience outweighing the discomfort of separation. Lucky parents and children find they can separate from each other, and beautifully, if they are genuinely motivated to do so. It is finding or developing the ability to change/separate that tunes one into the very heart of living. Learning to separate through dying by choice is, I discover, no exception.

It seems to me that no dying without assistance can be fully good. Partially good, but not fully so. I've thought a lot about the difference between dying by myself and dying while part of a bonded relationship. I've no doubt that I've grown able to do either well. But I've also no doubt that, single or bonded, whether a loner or not, assistance must always enhance dying. Assuming, of course, that the assistance is in the command of the dying person or someone she or he designates as a representative, and is given forthrightly with respect for the wishes of the person dying and without imposition against the will of the person who would die. Personal assistants are especially valuable when it comes to selecting one's date of exit. The earlier you focus upon establishing a date, the better refined its selection, and, of course, the better prepared you can be. Whenever you start, of course, the choice belongs to you, and you always have the freedom to adjust the date according to circumstances. In my view, you can't possibly start too early in life to specify a date.

Whatever length of time you give to establishing your date, it must be advantageous to have personal assistants weighing *your* questions with you. Perhaps they might challenge your initial choice of, say, age seventy-five, thinking you should aim for age one hundred, and so they might help you to seek your own level of awareness of your energy expenditure, stimulating you to think of whether you believe your life's energy is finite or not. If finite, you might then choose to channel it into the years between seventy-five and one hundred, conserving resources prior to age seventy-five for use in that period.

Surely if at an early age you are as attuned to the issues of planning a good death for yourself as you are attuned to the issues of planning your life span's content of education, career, family life, etc., you will have a far more clear perception of yourself by the time you reach your forties and fifties than you possibly could otherwise. With that advantage, you quite possibly would not suffer mid-life stress as it has been traditionally suffered. With your life's ending not being denied, with its being accepted and in preparation, you could enter your later life span with newfound fullness of living. You could make fullest use of your resources, relating more realistically to everyone as a person in a finite later life stage rather than as though you expect and want to extend your resources indefinitely. Surely, too, you would by then be part of one or more mutual assistance circles.

But what can you do if you are already in your forties or fifties? First of all, earnestly examine your attitudes in search of awareness of just how you are regarding the end of your life. Of course, you don't know exactly how you will die, but maybe you have a fantasy of what you

expect. Like it? Want to change it? You can. Reflect on
what your resources now are and are still becoming. How
differently would you use and enjoy your resources if
you knew you would ask yourself to spread them only to
age seventy-five versus indefinitely beyond that age? (I'm
not pushing age seventy-five. Eighty-five if you'd prefer,
or sixty-five! The choice of framing your life's canvas is
exclusively yours.) If you conclude you'd rather create
a good ending for yourself—out of the same self-respect
with which you chose to plan your family—then please
take heed. Lose no time before engaging whomever you
wish in open discussions of the value of suicide as a means
of creating a good death. Know that failure to develop
a comfortable circle of assistants by the time you are sixty
greatly increases the chance that you will have no command over your life's end, and so will die of the ravages
of illness or old age, following a period of waning rather
than fully lived life.

If you're in your sixties and can reach an unambivalent
decision that you want to take command of your life's
ending, then I'd like to suggest that you accept that the
odds are significantly against your developing or acquiring
assistants. On the grounds that your efforts to find assistants may fail, I think it would help if you set more store
in aiming to be your own assistant while, simultaneously,
seeking others apart from you. The important thing is not
to deprive yourself if you happen to be unable to elicit
help.

For you, then, it becomes critical to mobilize your own
most sharply focused thinking. I believe nothing will
activate your reflections more than discarding vague wondering about how one could know when to end life, replacing that by committing yourself in your own mind to
a specific date. If the thought of doing that paralyzes you,

it may be that your decision is still too ambivalent and you need to examine your feelings further.

Let's assume that you are in your late sixties, or even early seventies. You think you'd like to set a date, have wondered how you could ever know when. The problem with that approach is that it is locked into the assumption that suicide must be an act of impulse. It might help you to remind yourself that it is not an impulsive moment in your life for which you are looking, but, rather, a rational, fully calculated moment. Are you wed? Wasn't your wedding date set somewhat arbitrarily?

Think of being at a banquet where the board is heavily laden with marvelous foods. You have eaten your fill and a little more. A slight feeling of stuffed discomfort is with you. You know the supply of food is going to keep coming, and you feel your curiosity to taste each as it comes. Look at the people around you. Can you see that some have pushed themselves, feeling driven to taste everything, to eat every last morsel until they die sliding under the table in the agony of engorgement? Do the latter appear to you to be in an enviable state of ecstasy?

Try to look at your life in a parallel sort of way. Do you feel compelled to reach for every last breath? Or would you rather withdraw from life while you can do so comfortably? Perhaps obesity is to greed for food as senility is to greed for life.

IV

THE ART OF SUICIDE:
Notes from the Last Month of My Life

When, more than a decade ago, my early thinking about Exit House was taking shape, I thought it would be twenty-five to fifty years before public consciousness could be raised sufficiently for an Exit House to come into existence. In the interim, I've sensed the welling underground stream and come to believe it is bubbling at the surface so strongly now that we could have an Exit House within ten years. In the past few days it has dawned that an Exit House could be established now!

I sometimes imagine that I'm a millionaire. I will purchase a country estate or large town house in a state where aiding a suicide is not prejudged by state law to be criminal. I will hire a staff of persons who believe in the right to determine the length of one's own life. For the staff I will look for alert retired persons from the medical, legal, psychological, and social service professions. Or, for that matter, younger alert unretired professionals if they're ready to dare. Interested nonprofessionals will be welcomed for staff training. For a few months we will have workshops to clarify our resources and starting policies. We will consult community groups and try to elicit their support. We will study the inevitable opposition and aim to support its rights rather than to engage ourselves in battle with it. Then we will announce our readiness to provide counsel for persons interested in planning a self-determined good death for themselves. While for the time being we may not be able to provide the means for suicide, we will be glad to help clients know their best alternatives. Above all we will give clients our respect and our growing knowledge. Anyone contemplating suicide, rational or irrational, and of any age, would be welcomed to use our service. We would, of course, discourage irrationality and encourage rational contemplation and action.

We will try to develop ourselves as a model for other Exit Houses. We will aim for an economic structure that will both support our service at a high standard of quality and simultaneously provide service to people of any economic status.

I don't believe that children would become more suicidal than they already are if they found themselves living in a society which accepted and supported suicide as a basic human right. Quite the contrary. In such a mature society, I'd expect to find children less suicidal.

Suicides of children under eighteen would not automatically be ruled out at Exit House. However, they would not be assisted except in cases where an Exit House or hospital administration became convinced that the child was not capable of achieving a life satisfactory to self. The administration would hear adults who would protest child suicides. But they would not permit imposition of forced life upon any child, on the grounds that some people would not hesitate to force another person to live a life unsatisfactory to the self.

Jo in 1923, age 7.

Jo, age 15,
in her first
store bought dress.

College yearbook picture, c. 1937.

In 1939, Jo and Bill Wade had a proper wedding.

Jo, Timmy, Tommy, and Bill; c. 1943.

Jo, Timmy, and Tommy in 1944, just before they left for Alaska.

Jo and her second husband, Warren Caro; c. 1950.

Jo bundled against the Alaska winter.

Timmy and Tommy with the Ehrharts, their adoptive parents; c. 1950.

Jo receiving a Master of Social Service degree, June 1952.

Jo in Provincetown, 1968/1974.

Jo modeling jewelry she and a friend designed using objects found on the beach; c. 1974.

Jo and Mel Roman, 1974.

Jo working on her touch boxes,
and posing in front of
a finished series of them.

Jo as she appeared on videotape,
made shortly before
her suicide in June 1979.

I suppose there is inextricably entangled in these reflections the question of imposing life upon a child who is, say, so defective from birth that he or she will never be able to fend for himself or herself. Yes, I believe the child's parents ought be given the carefully administered right to act in the child's behalf to terminate the child's life; or perhaps the right to turn the child over to a group authorized to make and carry out such a decision; the freedom not to force life upon a child too defenseless to achieve a position of self-determination. Of course, opposition to such a development might be intense. On the other hand, although intense, it might be surprisingly small. Within the human mass there is, I believe, a vast sea of compassion yet to be developed.

We must guard against abuse, and sometimes we will be insufficiently on guard. But our limitations cannot justify either forcing or taking life against a person's will. And when a person is incapable of developing will, then who is to decide? Here we come to what I find to be a gray area. When a parent has a child who cannot be assured achievement of a useful level of will and self-determination, then that parent should be offered assistance in taking responsibility in the child's behalf for termination of that life. At the same time, it seems to me that parents must have the right to maintain their defective child if they wish. Still, I have trouble if I imagine being a child so defective that I could have no hope of fending for myself. Somehow I wish my fate would be left not exclusively to my parents and whatever need they might have to make themselves feel better by keeping me alive. I'd like to see a society which would make note of the existence of such children, and look for ways not only of preventing such human anomalies but also for ways of relieving them and their parents from forced living.

I recognize that an eighteen-year-old hasn't lived to weigh his or her values as has, say, a forty-year-old. I would have a society which honors the right to suicide make an accommodation which would reflect such awareness. I think it reasonable to conclude that anyone who has lived forty years—the normal life span prior to human intervention with nature—and has decided that is enough should be guaranteed assistance to a decent suicide within, say, twenty-four hours after request. (That twenty-four-hour leeway enables personnel to present alternatives to persons whose wish to commit suicide seems impulsive.) However, for would-be suicides between the ages of eighteen and forty, administering suicide programs might lengthen the time between the request for assistance and the actual exit date. Say, a month at the eighteen-year-old end of the spectrum and a week at the thirty-nine-year-old end.

I would make available on the market an Exit Pill specifically designed for swift, painless, irreversible death. I would have this pill and its purpose labeled fully, as clearly as are labels on other lethal materials openly available on the market—garden chemicals, household products, etc. It would not require a prescription. In my view, the ready availability of such a lethal pill would not lead to a terrible upsurge of suicides and homicides. It is not the availability of means which makes one decide to end his or her own or another's life. Certainly the unavailability of a decent means hasn't prevented suicides or homicides. That unavailability has only made those which do take place messier than necessary.

So if a decent Exit Pill becomes readily available on the market, what is the point of having suicide programs?

Among the many reasons, one of the more obvious ones is that it makes it possible for one to register intent and so simplify estate planning, reduce suspicion of fraud, etc. Far more importantly, thoughtful planning of a rational suicide is potentially—however paradoxical—a life-enriching experience. For some, it would certainly be so life-liberating as to provide reason for prolongation of life in situations where the wish for suicide isn't precipitated by intractable emotional or physical distress.*

I wish that on the day I walked out of the Guttman Institute with confirmation that I had a breast tumor I could have gone forthwith to a Rational Suicide Institute. There I would have told them that I imagined I might have cancer; that if I did and its treatment or course would make significant inroads on the quality of my life, I would want to make the earliest possible start at planning a suicide because I would not want to subject self or family to terminal cancer.

The staff would swing into action to help me alleviate the shock and pain of facing a potentially shortened life. They would help me clarify or learn how to clarify my medical options; how to find medical personnel who would also respect my right or else to elicit from a traditional doctor the information I'd need to assess what medical options I could apply to a life I would end this side of terminal pain rather than—as others might elect—after terminal pain set in, or never, thus leaving the timing

* It was Jo's feeling that knowing one always had the option would reduce impulsiveness. Further, it would enable the person to be fully responsible for the decision to live and perhaps thereby be able to live more vitally and meaningfully—all part of her philosophy that self-determination is an essential component of a responsible life.—M.R.

of my death to a contest between nature and the medical world's life-extending technology.

In my case, I think they would have helped me set a date quite similar to the one my family and I established by ourselves. And I suspect they would have learned that—given my suicide plan—there was no point at all in my subjecting myself (and those close to me) to the discomfort and cost of chemotherapy. Lacking an institute's assistance, I endured ten months of chemotherapy, which made awful inroads on my life's time and quality.

Imagine: You have come to a time when you are ready to die and would like to do so. You have the means to end your life in as comfortable and certain a way as you can devise in the absence of a well-researched Exit Pill.

You are seventy and of sound mind and generally good spirit. Your economic circumstances are such that while you can't live luxuriously, with Social Security you're managing all right, and you could maintain your life style for another decade or so. You have two grown children, who might supplement your Social Security to keep you similarly supported after eighty if you lived beyond that time. Most of your relatives have lived into their eighties and nineties, so you might too.

When family and friends gather for your seventieth birthday, everyone remarks on your vitality and voices expectations that you'll still be lively at eighty. And ninety. The younger the speaker, the more cheerful the tone. You feel yourself lucky. You laugh merrily and accept your plaudits. Yes, you do owe your physical fitness to your sturdy stock and your good habits of regular exercise and well-chosen nutrition. Yes, you enjoy numerous interests and still find your days too short for all you want to do.

Yes, you appreciate being recognized for your community service. Life, you say, has been good to you and you look forward to more.

Afterward you sit content and alone in the small new apartment you moved into a few years after your husband died. Even though it had hurt to leave the home you'd shared through the raising of the children, you hadn't minded terribly. It felt so sensible to take a smaller, more manageable space. And you can surround yourself with your sentimental treasure. You feel so cozy and aglow with the party's honor as you curl into your favorite chair. How good it feels to be quiet and alone.

As you sit reflecting you find yourself thinking less and less of the party's spirit and more and more about your eightieth birthday, a decade hence. Your eighty-year-old cousin had sat out your party in a corner, unable to hear much conversation through the babble, with a noticeable tremor of her head as each person politely spent a few moments with her. No one much cared to linger with her. Not that she was at all unpleasant. It was just that conversation didn't come easy with her. There seemed too little to talk about. One had to reach out—or rather back— into her past to find subjects to withstand verbal exchanges.

Your thoughts are riveted on your cousin because you remember that ten years ago you were instrumental in holding a seventieth-birthday party for her. Was she not then quite like you are now, lively and admired for being a stimulating person? Your cousin hasn't had any serious illness. How come she seems so faded? Could that happen to you? Zestful you?

Zestful you? You realize you feel tired. Naturally, after partying all afternoon! Maybe you'll go to bed early. Get up early tomorrow because you have so much to do. Your son calls. "Well, Mom, recovering from your party?" You venture to reveal you're wondering whether you'll be like your cousin in ten years. "Don't be ridiculous, Mom! Of course you won't be like her. You're going to be tap dancing at ninety!" You realize your question faces into an absolutely taboo subject. No one, not even your son, wants to hear your concern.

Why, in your generally open family, is your concern disallowed? It was lovely hearing all that praise today, but, come to think of it, its effusiveness was less for what you are doing than for the fact that you are doing all these things at seventy. And, come to think of it further, you understand part of that message because it is true that you couldn't be doing what you're doing—regardless of your healthful living—if in fact you weren't making a special effort to do so. Yes, part of the investment of your energy is, indeed, into behaving energetically against the image of being slowed. In private, you *do* rest more than you ever did. And when you are out and "doing," it *does* tax you more to walk with a spring in your step than it did not long ago. Perhaps you are disallowing your own concern.

You know very well you're not going to be tap dancing at ninety. Wouldn't even want to be. A wave of shame washes over you. Shame? Quickly you fill your mind with images of every nonagenarian you've ever known or heard of. You try to focus your imagery on ninety-year-olds whose minds are alert, who go to work every day, who are turned to for sage advice. You know you've seen or heard of them—or one or two—somewhere along the way, but where are they now? All you can see clearly are those merrily dancing people in the yogurt ads. No, you have no models for ninety and you don't really want to become a ninety-year-old model. Whatever for! Oh sure, if you could be ninety and truly alert and zippy. But you know in the marrow of your bones you have no such desire, no matter how often you've claimed you want to live forever—or at least to a hundred. Why do people—you!—say that? Why does it seem that one is expected to say that? Why does it seem to convey failure or irreverence for life if one doesn't have—or claim—an ambition to live forever?

It occurs to you that one reason you make such an effort to keep yourself perky isn't because you feel you'd be a failure if you ran out of verve. Rather, you don't know how long you're going to live, and if it happens that you live as long as your cousin . . . well, maybe you can ward off becoming that decrepit. Maybe. Exercise. Nutrition. Thank goodness you're an active person. Maybe you can keep regenerating yourself.

Maybe. And what if "it" keeps coming? You notice, as you're sitting, how you're rubbing your hands. Those stiffening joints. Images of elderly people kicking up their heels have been replaced with images culled from memories of TV programs buoying hopes of relief for arthritics. Gnarled painful joints being replaced miraculously by plastic miracles. No, one must not allow oneself to anticipate becoming unbearably arthritic. One mustn't! One must never give up hope! Cures are always arriving. Besides, it won't happen to you. Or will it? Isn't it already happening? Didn't you send for the government pamphlets on arthritis, read all their hope hype, and learn there is naught but aspirin for you until your arthritis gets much worse? Didn't your doctor minimize your pain, which has been creeping into your joints for the last several years? Isn't it true that you're disinclined to mention to anyone that such signs of old age are advancing?

You mustn't think of growing old. Seventy! Mustn't think

of growing old! It's unmentionable. Praise is for being younger, not older. You don't look seventy! they say, conveying that it would be awful if you did. You feel it's somehow inappropriate to take pride in looking younger than most women your age, or pride in being self-sufficient, in finding small pleasures in life, in not being a burden to others. (Heaven forbid!)

You reflect on all this. You are seventy and of sound mind and generally good spirit.

You have come to a time when you are ready to die and would like to do so.

I do not wish to invest my energy in defending my position against the opposition. Rather, I would like to acknowledge the inevitable presence of opposition. I would not ask that it be otherwise. I respect the rights of opponents, as long as they do not infringe upon my rights. I would help them extend their own lives as long as they wish, under whatever conditions might prevail for them. All I ask is that they be restrained from imposing their point of view upon others—especially me. I want each of us to have the right to live and to die in our own way and time.

Further, I want to express appreciation of the opposing position. It is good to have one's thinking constantly challenged. The opponents are very helpful in pointing out issues and the cutting edges of responsibility and change. It is good to listen to all religious and philosophical convictions. The voice of opposition to my position may be immediate and strident. But if one dares listen for quieter voices—particularly the inner voices of the heart and mind—I believe there is an important hum welling. If your own life circumstances and associations are such that what you hear is only dominant opposition and if you care to put your weight behind freedom of choice, let me suggest that you devote a day or two to the following exercise. Locate the best nursing home or hospice that you can, as well as an institution for defective humans. I urge that your approach be one of respect and appreciation that for the most part the people who staff these homes and institutions are dedicated to service. At the same time, being human, they will want you to see them at their best.

Their best will be some combination of what they imagine you would be pleased to see and what they personally believe it would be good of them to be doing. Generally, staff conduct can be expected to reflect traditional, socially approved attitudes. This would mean presenting an image of a well-tended place where the residents are maintained in a clean and orderly fashion. Once you are shown beyond the lobby, chances are you would be shown a section of the residence where the most capable residents live, i.e., residents who can help keep themselves clean and who are able to specify when they are in need of assistance.

You might or might not want to go beyond this area. If you asked to see other areas of the residence, you might or might not be shown. But do ask to be shown where disoriented or senile or emotionally or physically incompetent children or adults are maintained. If you get into such areas, ask yourself how you would feel about being there. Even if you would not like to be there, suppose you had to be. Do you think you'd feel free to tell staff what you felt or wanted? Would you be free to protest? Who would decide what is best for you, you or the staff? Suppose you decided you'd had enough of living and would like to die? Would they hear you? If so, would they help you die? If you said that you'd like to die, would the staff interpretation be that they are failing you; that a visitor hearing you might think the staff is failing you; that you are feeling deranged? Would they drug you to prevent your expressing your wish to die? Would they regard your behavior as provocative and move you away from where visitors might hear you? If you grew faint, and might die, would they give you a pacemaker?

But, you ask, are not the odds against my or my loved ones ever being so confined? The odds are getting smaller and smaller. Whenever you hear of the wonders resulting from medical technology, remember that for every person enabled to live a longer life or even a better one than he or she could without such development, there are many more having lives extended into institutions. When you hear about the decreasing need for hospital beds, remember that a whole new industry of nursing homes and hospices is replacing those beds. Also, that growing numbers of people are living extended lives in the community but under control of tranquilizers and other drugs. And above all remember that if you give your life over to the life extenders, you relinquish your own control of your life and increase the likelihood that part of your life will be spent institutionalized or drugged. You will find yourself monitored by people committed to prevention of your death unless medical authorities dare to declare that they can do no more to extend your life—a situation still rare, and likely to occur only where hospices have fought themselves into existence. Hospices—as they are coming into existence now—simply had to emerge in our times. They are the forefront of resistance to life extension in our time. They are the forefront of resistance to life extension for all people at all costs. They have met with extensive opposition, but slowly they have been born. Their growth is a promising development and marvelous reassurance against forced life extension for a handful of terminally ill patients.

There should be more hospices for people who are ready to die and want to go through the dying process with the alleviation of pain being the only human intervention.

We must develop Exit Houses for people who are ready to die and want to take responsibility for the time and nature of their demise.

I've created for myself an accepting community of people ready to assist me in a responsible ending of my life. As I write, there are more than one hundred people who know of my suicide intent. Still more who know of my philosophy regarding suicide as a human right to be established. Because I had engaged so many in open discussion, I was in the advantageous position of being able to select from among the larger number those who were most open to the possibility of assisting me. But it turned out that had nothing to do with my selection of assistants. My private circle of assistants was drawn first from persons who happened to be in the vicinity of my needs as they occurred upon emergence of my cancer and upon the concommitant advancement of my suicide date.

The first people to whom I turned were unaware of my history of interest in the subject of suicide. And I had no informed view of their attitudes. Heretofore, whenever I had broached the subject of suicide with anyone it was colored distinctly by timidity of approach. It was as though I expected reactions of dismay or rejection. I wanted to elicit consideration but approached strictly defensively. However, once my suicide was near at hand I needed assistance fast and certain and could not afford shilly-shallying. I needed to place consideration of myself and those close to me at the forefront. My primary concern was no longer weighing with others the pros and cons of suicide or aiming to raise their consciousness. Whatever their views, I must work with theirs and mine to create useful assurance. Timidity was replaced by temerity.

My first action to elicit assistance came with my new medical team, all strangers to me. In my very first meeting with each of them I openly stated that I regarded my life as belonging to me. I wanted them to respect my right to determine what treatment I would or would not accept. I was keenly interested to know from them what my medical alternatives would be. However, I was not interested in having them impose upon me their views of what quality of life I should or should not live with. I wanted them to know that I positively would end my life before undergoing terminal cancer. Therefore, whatever they would tell me about my medical options should be in the framework not of extending my life regardless of quality, but, rather, of helping me find whether there was any medical care which could permit me to have a life of such quality, physically, that I would regard it as worth living. I stressed that I was the only person with the right to make the final assessment, but that I needed their assistance to make the best calculations of my probabilities.

My declaration was met with much blankness of eye. I was both amazed and strengthened by my audacity. From the outset I sensed that I had entered a new realm of suicide consideration. While I still truly cared about what the other person was feeling and I felt the pain of rejection, the burden of weighing their views had shifted to them. It was my responsibility to see to it that the doctor's view of suicide would neither interfere with my thoughtful planning nor distort the medical information the doctor was being paid to provide.

I rejected the service of several doctors whose blank stares felt impenetrable. Finally, I found one who had enough openness of communication that he exclaimed in a concerned, rather than rejecting, manner, "You're suicidal!" At last I had an opening to another human being. Given his response, dialogue was possible. The twenty minutes allowed for the session was very constraining, but even a little dialogue seemed to have great potential value. No, I explained, I am not suicidal even though, yes, I will commit suicide. I love life and have several projects I especially want to complete. I had been counting on having at least a decade in which to do so. Now, with the cancer, it appeared that I could no longer count on that decade. I needed his assistance not to give me hope of living a decade consumed by cancer treatment. Rather, I needed his assistance to help me calculate the longest period of time I could count on of good-quality time—by my standards. I was not asking him to play God and to divine the date of my death, nor to play at defeating God by extending my life beyond God's will, nor to tell me how long and under what circumstances I ought to live. I appreciated that he could not know absolutely the course my cancer would take, but I was sure he could clarify both the statistical odds and treatment possibilities and probabilities. Whether or not he could or would, that was the information I wanted to buy in order to calculate for myself the longest life possible before the onset of terminal disease. For the quality of my life to be satisfactory, I would have to condense my decade's worth of projects into a shorter time. From a medical point of view, could I count on having five years at the typewriter? If I counted on five, how high would the risk be that terminal pain might cut off the last chapter of *Exit House*? I didn't want him to calculate how long I could live. Rather, I wanted him to give me the information needed in order to do my own calculations. How long did he feel it was safe for me to count on being comfortable enough to work every day?

I could see the doctor's struggle in his eyes. He had enough respect for me and self-confidence not to avert his look. Could I really count on him to level with me? This stranger? This man in his late sixties, with years of indoctrination to extend life at all cost and to deny suicide? Our twenty minutes together included physical examination and discussion of medical factors quite apart from our between-the-lines minuscule dialogue on suicide. I could feel hope not only because he permitted the dialogue (of course, the control was his), but because, to my amazement, he had dared to give me information other doctors must have known and withheld, hiding behind the absence of test data. This doctor's respect and confidence enabled him to share wth me his initial impression that my tumors were malignant. Sure that speculation was distressing. But the gift of rapport cushioned all. I left with my heart pounding, fear choking, tears welling, and all this made bearable because I felt hope for forthright communication with someone who had the medical information I needed in order to make the best plan for my life. My probably shortened life.

So it was that my first assistant came into my circle, in spring 1978, early in my treatment. He came reluctantly. And, across the next months, unevenly. Always needing to be coaxed and reassured by me. He accepted my right to establish the length of my life span. (I had set the date by then.) He admitted that the debilitating chemotherapy I had undergone for ten months was not necessary to keep me functioning until summer 1979. He did ask if I meant to exit in early or late summer, and when I said my calculation led me to aim for early summer, he seemed better enabled to accept my discontinuing therapy.

I would like to name my doctor and credit him with coming to respect my right to determine my life's quality, content, and length. But, having reached my conclusion more via ferreted responses and innuendo than directly, until the very last meeting with him, and believing his colleagues might well berate him for his openness and degree of acceptance, I find myself inclined to protect his privacy by not publishing his name.

In my last contact with him, he confirmed that there was no significant basis beyond blind and routine hope to expect my cancer's course to allow me even one more day of decent quality as long as chemotherapy continued. While chemo might keep me alive longer, it absolutely would continue to diminish the quality of my life. He accepted my right to opt for a short period of undrugged, high-quality living against a longer period of life constantly burdened with the discomforts, preoccupations, and costs of treatment. He volunteered to spare me further discussion with my chemotherapist. I had long since stopped trying to reach the latter, as he seemed so distressed by my stance that I feared interference with his skill in injecting the chemicals.

Perhaps having my position in writing alleviated any fear my doctor might have had that he could be held liable for my act of suicide. In any event, I do recommend a well-thought-through written statement—keep a copy! —to make certain your doctor understands your position and the nature of your questions.

How do you see the landscape of your life? How like your dreams is it being and becoming? Before you started school you were probably quite capable of weighing profound questions about what would be the major events in your life. How often were you encouraged to use your mind to shape yourself? To plan your play, your study, your work, your family?

Were you helped to dream about and plan your death? If you weren't, when you view your landscape you will find a very blind spot at its end; find that your play, study, work, and living are oriented unrealistically to an open-endedness of eternal embodied life which you are not about to have.

Think of how important it is when you go on vacation to be able to gauge your activity in accordance with how much time you may reasonably allow yourself. Think of what a difference it makes in studying or working when you can pace yourself by knowing whether you have, say, eight hours or must keep working without an end in sight. Think of the difference to your family life when you take responsibility for planning what time you will give to it.

True, there are times when you'd like to have more time than allotted. But aren't you usually able to pace yourself so that you've done enough within the allotted time? Enough and better? And when you find you need a little more time, aren't you often able to arrange to have it exactly because thoughtful structuring enhances flexibility?

The issue of the right to die would not exist if it were not for medical use of technology in developing life extension.

It may seem fanciful sci-fi to envision high-rise buildings filled with vaults containing electrically supported human life. Whole bodies and body parts. But if it is possible—as it nearly is—why not? I wouldn't protest. They may even have my body parts. As long as lives of others aren't jeopardized, why shouldn't someone be free to try to extend her or his life as long as possible, or to alter it along the way? Face lifts, organ transplants, transsexual transformations, whatever. As an artist, I'm the last person to discourage human creativity. I only ask that I always have protected my own fullest freedom to choose whether I want to participate in someone else's creativity, and be protected from having someone else's will imposed upon me. I ask the same for you.

I have no quarrel whatsoever with humankind's inclination to extend earthly life. On the contrary, I admire and marvel at our inventiveness. I love the fact that human endeavor has enabled me to live beyond the original human life span.

As I write, it is the 1979 of your landscape; the beginning of the final sixty-seven days of mine. I feel like an astronaut looking at the earth from a distance and seeing absurdities and potentials in raw perspective. I want to call out to you to see what I see.

We and our doctors have become strangers to one another, as separated from the human factor as are the high-altitude bomber and his target. In the doctors' favor we can say at least that they mean well. Does the bomber tell himself the same? I am not suggesting it is the doctor's responsibility to solve our dilemma, any more than I think it is the bomber's responsibility that we have war. Neither war nor wanton extension of life without regard for quality can be resolved by anyone except ourselves. Historically, it appears we are not very good at resolving such problems once they exist. When a new powerful factor is born, it tends to become entrenched in the blindness of the environment and so to gain a foothold before its negative impact can be offset.

WHAT A PARADOX IT IS that
> the more we claim human life to be eternal, declare reverence for human life, and express the wish to extend embodied human existence ever beyond mankind's original life span of, say, forty years;
>
> the more we erode our ecological resources, the more voracious become our appetites for war.

WHEREAS, I find,
> confrontation with alternative of global suicide —made a reality by the hydrogen bomb born in our time—precipitates
>> human containment of its drive to war, and makes more accessible the acceptance of human mortality expressed in readiness to take responsibility for creating constructive ending.

Are we agreed that everyone has a right to live? That you have a right to live? To live as you wish as long as you endanger no one? That society is obliged to recognize and protect that right? The recognition of such a basic right and the laws protecting it were not carved in granite when humankind was born. Recognition of the right and then the protective laws evolved slowly. In fact, the ever-changing human condition and the ever-present gray areas of our living still render us incapable of absolute commitment. Around the globe we still engage in taking the lives of others, readily rationalizing our acts. Our protective laws and their application vary substantially from country to country and within any country.

In the event that you stepped into an area where your right to live was not respected, apart from wishing for a social structure to protect you, I daresay you'd make a fight for that right despite failure of others to recognize your right and to provide protective service.

Can we be agreed that everyone has a right to die? That you have a right to die? To die as you wish as long as you endanger no one? That society is obliged to recognize and protect that right? The recognition of such basic right and the laws to protect it *were* carved in granite when humankind was born. Erosion has blurred the inscription.

Depending upon the circumstances into which a child grows, it is highly probable that a child will find surrounding adults trying to color the child's perception, considerations, and so the belief systems which the child eventually uses to shape itself.

As a child, you were probably capable of contemplating your life span and getting under way with the task of shaping its content. Before you could start school, you probably had formed answers for the common questions about your future. And you could indicate your perception of a time frame by saying when you would start school, when you'd be grown up, that eventually you'd grow old and die. Regardless of your ability to conceptualize, it is also probable that your responses were dominated by the views of your environment, especially your parents. Chances are they consciously wanted you to develop their belief systems, and conveyed unspoken attitudes to you as well. So if you were born in America before, say, 1940, the initial shaping of your life span might have been for you to stay at home until you married, to have four children, to be a doctor or fireman when you grew up. You wouldn't question religious, political, or other beliefs your parents wanted you to share. If you happen to have been born later, chances are that you were subjected to a revised group of questions and mind-shapings so that before starting school you could have depicted your life course as one in which you would become a doctor or a fireperson or astronaut. You might not choose to marry. Whether or not you'd marry, you might have children.

As you contemplate your life's landscape, I urge you to note the blind spot you probably have when you look at your life's end. Yes, of course, you know you will die. You may have become aware of death before you did of sex.

Look at how society encouraged you, from all directions, to be very mindful of all major life events and to dream of them in advance, in detail, so as to be best prepared. How old were you when you began dreaming, thinking, talking, and planning about the important events of your life?

Today we know as little about attitudes and behavior related to suicide as we did about sex before Kinsey dared open the door for us around 1950. All the sexual blindness that existed before then continues to exist in large measure throughout the world, but the world will never be the same because consciousness has been raised and alternatives have been born. People are free to remain in the closet or to step into the light of day. I believe our understanding of suicide has a similar transformation emerging. Closeted in our culture, suicide is regarded remarkably the same as was sex. Not to be talked about. Shameful.

Why not calculate and create for yourself and those close to you a life span from which you may all benefit? Talk openly with your spouse, children, best friends about how long you would really like to live and under what conditions, under what conditions you'd rather not live so long. Learn limits they would establish for themselves. Don't diminish one another by dismissing the subject with a simple declaration that you want to live forever or until one hundred or some other improbability. Press yourselves to be as specific as possible as to your preferences and probabilities.

Quickly: How many decades do you expect to live?

Reflectively: How many decades do your relatives tend to live? Have you any reason to think your wishes or life style will cause you to live longer? Shorter?

Imagine yourself at twenty. At thirty. At forty. At fifty. At sixty. At seventy. At eighty. At ninety. At one hundred. Are you familiar with any centenarians? Would you like such a life for yourself? Is your life style directed to such a life span?

Imagine yourself at the oldest age which you believe you probably *could* reach. What quality of life would be essential for you to be truly glad to be alive on a day-to-day basis?

Are you telling yourself it is not possible to weigh these matters because of all the unknown variables? When you were a child, did the unknown variables of the future prevent you from reflecting on, say, whether and when you'd marry or preparing yourself for other eventualities of relevance to your life?

I suspect the reasons people haven't commonly taken command of their life spans' end are manifold and that there are significant variations among families, cultures, and times. Suicide has been an honorable and traditional life closure in some cultures. In other cultures and times it has been more rigidly opposed than presently in our Western civilization.

When someone commits suicide, the more rational it is, the more likely it is to be artfully concealed.

Even if you don't think of yourself as an artist—a painter, say—you probably can imagine how different it would feel if you had a choice between spending your time painting on a roll of canvas which is slowly unrolling versus painting on a large canvas whose edges are delineated by you. In either instance you have a goal of creating, if not a masterpiece, the very best painting you possibly can. You understand that when your painting is finished, your bodily life will simultaneously come to its end.

The slowly unrolling canvas—you have no control over its movement—will come to an end, you know, but you have no idea when. Unless you are accidentally killed, you will just keep on painting until the canvas runs out. Since you cannot know when that will be, there is no way you can organize your painting. You cannot plan to make its final stroke. Your painting may prove to be beautiful, but you cannot claim it as your creation because you will have had to leave its final stroke to the happenstance of forces other than your own.

If you establish your canvas's boundary and face the same task of creating the very best painting you possibly can, you may not paint a masterpiece or even a beautiful canvas, but you will at least have created a painting by the simple determination of making the painting's final stroke.

Every day it becomes more probable—even if you try to anticipate the arriving end of the unrolling canvas, becoming hypersensitive to its slowing or uneven pace; even if you think you're ready at a moment's notice to make that final stroke—that the odds against your winning are increasing. You stand before the canvas, waiting and wanting to strike, perhaps tired of your effort, perhaps aching in old bones. Locked in a dilemma. Suppose you strike and the canvas keeps unrolling and you've no more paint. Are you prepared to join ranks with all the bodies locked into assorted stances before still unrolling canvases, unable to break the monotony of the seemingly endless white? To be pulled from there into basket weaving? Into being steered mindlessly or drugged or against your protests into eating or being infused with body nourishment and extension? Is such an alternative better or worse than the alternative of withholding a final gesture so that at least you can have your own stroking to watch on the canvas of your mind as long as you have a body to sustain it?

You would find, if you looked, no concretely established rights and an utter confusion of laws concerning suicide from state to state and country to country. The laws are so loose-toothed that they serve primarily as a source of anxiety for those who would commit or aid a rational suicide. The laws appear to have survived primarily to guard against suicide as a concealment of homicide or for criminal intent, such as to defraud an estate. In a few places there are archaic laws which state suicide to be illegal, but these specific laws are rarely applied. Prosecution of a person attempting suicide or assisting a suicide is rarely undertaken. Incarceration of a person attempting suicide is more common, but nowadays the person is likely to be homicidal as well as suicidal. Incarceration or prosecution when a person is perceived as rational is highly unlikely. Still, any danger whatsoever of incarceration or punishment must be felt as a deterrent to one who would commit suicide. Especially if one is concerned with the well-being of survivors who would have to bear the brunt of such a stigma.

We, society, seem to be saying that there must be some unforgivable guilt attached to the willful ending of a life—even one's own.

I feel deeply indebted to my forebears who used their own lives to create and to spread at large the realization that humankind's survival and maturation hinges on clarifying and establishing individual rights to self-determination. I'm embarrassed that I've taken these rights so lightly. Belatedly, I see that rights are hard won and constantly in need of protection. Further, that their underpinnings and the environments in which rights emerge are in such a never-ending state of flux that rights need constant clarification and updating.

My embarrassment stems from the feeling that some-

how I might have brought more particularly useful reinforcement out of my own life experiences. I had the
luck of discovering early the danger to my personality as
people of divergent views competed to impose their views
on me, aiming to diminish my self-determination. It doesn't
matter that each group—primarily religious groups—was
extremely earnest and well-meaning. Even loving. The
truth is that each needed to regard its own view as the best
or the correct view, each was disinclined to measure its
view against others, each wanted to shape—some to pos-
sess—my mind.

We all know our lives can be snuffed out in a flash,
romantically while doing something we enjoy, or tragically
in some crushing accident, or gently in our sleep. We can
also know that the odds are against such swift deaths.
Probably most readers will be confronted with some
period of life when they will be aware of being actively
in the process of dying. Depending upon the circumstances and personalities, some significant portion of living
will then be absorbed either with denial or with making
a good dying. Each according to her or his own standards.
Each out of her or his living time. People, things, and
places of life will be regarded in new perspective. I believe
those perspectives can be enhanced by advance considerations.

In the light of my own present living and dying perspective, for example, I can see that the place I now
choose for my dying is rather different from what it would
have been if, say, I was dying ten years ago. I was more
dependent then than I am now and would have been more
in need of approval and assurances from others. Handholding and the love of others is still deeply important to me,

but dying alone is no longer ominous. Then I'd have thought more of romantic settings such as a moonlit dune, whereas now I treasure more the comfort of home. On the other hand, were I alone at this stage of my life, without intimate family and friends, without a home setting shared with another, I imagine I would welcome as a first choice a comfortable way of closing my home and moving into a comfortable place for dying such as that which a community-built Exit House could provide—a place where I could have comfortable final visits with family and friends, where our shared needs could be tended, where I could be assured swift painless death at the moment of my choice. Perhaps if such existed, even now while having this loving setting with my family, I think I might prefer to die there. I think an Exit House separate from my home could be inviting and better in many ways for family, friends, and me. While I'm profoundly happy to have a real Exit House at home, I'd be happier still if I had a choice between my home Exit House and a community-provided Exit House. I think of Exit House as a place to serve the living. A place which uniquely incorporates the dying of persons who are ready to end their lives. A place which enhances public awareness of its life/death cycle and the cycle's nourishment of our planet. A place where song and laughter and ordinariness and creativity blend with and ease sorrows.

The existence of Exit House need not argue nor interfere with the existence of other, differing perceptions. No need to rule out traditional attitudes toward life and death. No need to press anyone to choose either death by happenstance or death by choice. The option has always been and always will be present. People have always made their choice of how to end their lives. But, heretofore, blindly. Now, no longer blindly. Or at least less so.

I keep thinking I ought to prefer to die in my own home Exit House rather than at a community Exit House. But, oddly, I don't feel that way, much as I deeply love our home. For a while I thought I might be harboring some feeling that my dying at home might sort of "contaminate" the place for my husband, somehow make it more difficult for him to have the option of living here without me. As though some afterimage of my lifeless body in our bed might be haunting. Spooky? Perhaps something of those things. But I think not really. I feel strong aversion to dying in a hospital or a strange place. But there's something so respectful in Exit House as I envision it, something so hospitable and accommodating and clearly focused on making the time of dying the very best possible experience in accordance with the wishes of the dying, that I can't help but feel I'd actually rather die there than at home. Now isn't that something! I can feel just how real the contribution of Exit House's atmosphere and service would be. Of course, to be there I'd have to have walked away from the familiarity of my home setting. And I'd be meeting my family and friends away from my home turf. At Exit House that would feel good. Somehow, even preferable. That's remarkable, I think.

I peek in upon myself now in my dying and am simply awed—tongue-tied, too—at the sight of my untapped potential, the lodes of resources grown rich through my life and about to die with me. I weep with sorrow—less for myself (that too!) than for this world of human beings

who are, as I, unnecessarily crippled because we live in
a world which has not come to respect our worth.

It would be easy to think I'm projecting blame from my
childhood deprivation, but I believe I'm far past such
reaction when I point to the need to free children from
being possessed by their elders. A distinction must be
made between possession of children and responsibility
for them or love of them. It is a critical distinction and too
easily overlooked. We thought our child labor laws were
a breakthrough. Well, they are important—even though
only a small fraction of earth children are protected by
them. But they count for a mere smidgen against all that
needs doing to free children: to protect them from mind-
bending co-optation by their elders; to enable them to discover and bring forth themselves.

I do believe there are such exciting things to do to
enrich the quality of human life. And imagine! Imagine
how different would be our exploration of life extension
and space development if we could just postpone our
urges to extend life until we have a universally good life
quality! We really could aim for a time when essentially
no one need have his or her life taken or prolonged against
his or her will; when children would be encouraged to
discover themselves, protected from having belief systems
imposed upon them, and enabled to perceive their life
spans as their own responsibility.

What a paradox that respect for suicide is a stepping-
stone. I suppose because it is just one more emerging right
to be recognized and secured along humankind's route to
humaneness.

V

EXIT HOUSE: A FANTASY

EXIT HOUSE

*A Manual
and Training Guide*

Contents

BACKGROUND

The Federal Commission of Death by Choice was established by the United States Congress in an extraordinary action on February 3, 1982. The Commission was charged with the responsibility for developing "a model for dignified death by suicide or euthanasia." Since no state volunteered accommodation for the effort, the Congress ordered the State of New York to provide essential adaptation of its laws and to provide protection for related personnel and facilities.

For some years prior, the suicide rate in many parts of the world had been steadily rising at a rate even more rapid than the rate of population growth. Efforts to control population growth appeared to bring about modification. Efforts to stem the tide of suicides, however, seemed only to exacerbate the trend and, simultaneously, to trigger turmoil. The United States had almost the world's highest suicide rate and unequaled stringency of punitive laws, despite the evidence of their uselessness as deterrent. But the 1980s suicidal persons simply planned

their deaths more cautiously. They also understood that
detention facilities were so overflowing with persons
charged with assault that the exclusion of suicidal persons
from incarceration was almost certain. The very few people actually arrested for suicidal attempts were almost
invariably simply handed a sedative or a tranquilizer capsule. Unless some self-inflicted injury required hospitalization, the person was promptly released and no effort was
made to require ingestion of the medication. Follow-up
studies comparing suicidal persons admitted to hospitals
for treatment (whether physical or psychological or combined) with those reported but not admitted to hospitals
showed essentially no difference in the percentage of persons subsequently making another attempt. The studies
showed, however, that subsequent attempts tended to be
more successful and more thoughtful.

By 1981 virtually every state legislature and Congress
was embroiled in heated debate. The major focus was in
New York State. Its legislature had actually passed a bill
abolishing punishment and providing funds for suicide-
prevention clinics, but the Governor had vetoed the bill,
declaring it intolerably costly and of doubtful effectiveness.
The Governor had urged passage of a bill simply abolishing legal restrictions. The solidly organized antiabortion
forces (known as AAF) within the state argued that re-
moval of restrictions would be tantamount to sanctioning
destruction of human life.

Just when the legislators were trying to close up for the
1981 Thanksgiving–Christmas recess, a counterforce to the
AAF, the national organization of SLIM (Self-Limiting
Movement) unleashed a carefully planned nationwide pro-
motion of live television interviews with articulate elderly
and painfully dying people who could think of no better
Christmas present than the privilege of release from tor-

tured lives. Thus pressured, but confident of the Governor's veto, the AAF permitted the country's first "pro-suicide" bill to pass.

In this tense climate, the New York legislature was hardly pleased with Congress's 1982 charge to them. Still, their selection by Congress had not been arbitrary. New York State was, in fact, further along in its considerations of euthanasia than most other states; it had demonstrated better than average capacity to control the excesses of its legislative body. Open brawling and even gunshots had marked debate in other states. Many lawmakers throughout the land were inclined toward bodyguards because of their publicized positions on euthanasia. As Congress debated the subject and considered selecting one state to be charged with responsibility, most states organized plans to secede, threaten to secede, or to join forces with other states in opposition. Assignment to the District of Columbia had been considered because it cannot secede, but was rejected for obvious symbolic reasons. The seeming impasse was broken when the Mayor of New York City facetiously but publicly suggested that the city could solve its financial plight of dependence on the state legislature's "mini-money-mercy" by getting Congress to make it the fifty-first state in exchange for willingness to administer a Rational Death program.

Amid the jokes and overwrought statements which followed, an idea emerged and was supported by a surprisingly large number of New York City residents and, remarkably, by each of its congressional representatives. The idea was that by assigning the responsibility to New York State there would indeed be an "out" in the event that local protest would threaten to get out of hand. New York City really could be made a separate state, on special terms which Congress could require. There were not only the aforementioned signs that New York City could accept this role without unmanageable upheaval, but it appeared it might be uniquely suitable. The presence of the United Nations and the clear international interest in the subject of Rational Death suggested that the burden of the study and developments might even be shifted eventually from American to international shoulders.

As New York State accepted its charge to adapt laws in support of a Rational Death program within its boundaries, it was already agreed that the program would be restricted to New York City and that full financial support would be granted by the federal government. Further, New York City was granted numerous other benefits as incentive, such as increased funds for housing. Most forcefully, the federal government took the position that it would accept New York City as the fifty-first state if New York State failed to enable the Rational Death program to have prompt state legislative support. This federal position provided the essential clout—despite the distaste of most New York State residents for financially supporting their brothers and sisters in New York City, they understood well that New York State's stature and welfare would suffer extreme loss if it gave up the distinction of New York City.

By September 1982, the Federal Commission on Rational Death had acquired, remodeled, and staffed the Peace Building overlooking the United Nations grounds and the East River. At opening ceremonies it was officially designated as the Federal Rational Death Studies Building. But by January 1983, when it opened its experimental services to the residents of New York City, it had become known simply as Exit House.

DEFINITION OF RATIONAL DEATH (Death by Choice)

In the Exit House manual and in general use by the Federal Commission of Death by Choice the term "Rational Death" refers exclusively to two types of death, namely:

1. Self-Termination (ST), in which a person's death is brought about deliberately by the person, by his own hand (i.e., not administered by another person),

2. Termination by Euthanasia (TE), in which death is brought about by Exit House personnel licensed to administer Euthanasia. Persons being terminated participate in the decision-making, if able to.

ORGANIZATIONAL STRUCTURE

The Federal Commission of Death by Choice is housed at 100 First Avenue, New York City, overlooking the East River. Its premises and programs are popularly, and hereafter, referred to under the caption of Exit House. Several wooded acres of Staten Island also belong to Exit House, but the central aspects of its work are all at its Manhattan headquarters.

The Commission's administrative offices and council chambers are located on several of the upper floors. Each of the nine Commission members has a separate office. Several larger chambers allow for various group meetings, hearings, and conferences. The Commission is responsible for overseeing all operations related to Exit House. Secretarial services are located at various offices and in a "pool" on the floor below.

The Research Division is housed on the two floors immediately above the administrative office—symbolizing, perhaps, the importance attached to the study of the Exit House program. The findings of the research personnel will be the basis for future developments. Every effort is made to employ the best-qualified researchers. They must study in depth the condition of Self-Termination (with and without Euthanasia) as experienced at Exit House with similar conditions outside, and they must study public attitudes toward Self-Termination and Euthanasia. They must make their findings available and must make recommendations to Exit House and the public.

The Library is housed on the top two floors (where there is also a lounge and dining room and its service areas). Sections of the Library are available to the public and a separate section is for authorized personnel only. (Confidential portions of library materials are sealed in a basement vault.) The lounge and dining facilities are available to the public which uses the library. The Library includes all possible related literature plus records of every termination certified by Exit House.

The Roof Garden includes landscaped areas, a pool, and a gymnasium.

The Public Relations Department is housed on the second floor (accessible by escalator from the lobby). This department handles direct dealings with the nonapplicant public. It prepares and distributes relevant literature, provides information and stimulation for media, etc.

The Legal Division occupies three of the lower floors. It has several sections. One handles all issues regarding insurance. Another, litigations. Licensing for Euthanasists is the focus of one section; matters relating to monetary and property bequests of Exiters, another. Still another focuses on bequests for transplants. And another on various aspects of body disposition. A series of Euthanasia Courtrooms occupies a full floor.

The Exit House Foundation distributes all funds directed to Exit House by way of grants, bequests, and donations.

The Training School, a State-accredited institution, occupies the next four lower floors. It trains students, regardless of their educational background, as Counselors, Caretakers, and researchers in the special subjects related to Self-Termination and Euthanasia. The school is the only place where persons can be trained and qualified as Euthanasists.

The Service Division occupies the ground floor of Exit House plus the low annexed building extension which winds through the landscaped grounds. The Service Division has two departments: the Department of Self-Termination and the Department of Euthanasia. Each of these is served by four common services: Home, Emergency, Referral, and Disposition Services. The extension houses all the counseling rooms—known as Exit Rooms—meditation rooms, a medical center, a staff lounge and swimming pool, the Caretakers' Center, a round-the-clock coffee shop, and rest rooms. On the main building's first floor are located the remainder of the Service facilities: Home, Emergency, Social, and Disposition Consultation Center. The basement houses the usual building-maintenance facilities and a garage, as well as storage vaults for confidential files and the facilities for dispatching bodies to the Rational Death Woods in Staten Island.

ASSORTED NOTES ON DESIGN OF EXIT ROOMS

Exit Rooms are designed in suites so they may be comfortably used as living spaces by one of two Counselors working with one Exiter and related persons. They are adaptable for work with Exiting couples, and in times of

PHYSICAL PLANT

Manhattan

Administration Building and Extension in Domed Gardens
(From top to bottom of building)

Floor No.

<table>
<tr><td>Elevators
Stairs</td><td>16</td><td>Roof Garden, Pool, Gym</td></tr>
<tr><td></td><td>15</td><td>Library</td></tr>
<tr><td></td><td>13–14</td><td>Research</td></tr>
<tr><td></td><td>11–12</td><td>Commission's Administrative Offices and Consultation Rooms, Business Offices, Secretarial Services</td></tr>
<tr><td></td><td>8–9–10</td><td>{ Legal Offices and Courtrooms
{ Exit House Foundation</td></tr>
<tr><td></td><td>5–6–7</td><td>Training School</td></tr>
<tr><td></td><td>4</td><td>Public Relations</td></tr>
<tr><td></td><td>2–3</td><td>Social Service and Nonresident Counselors</td></tr>
</table>

Ground Floor:

Main Building:

Lobby

Caretakers' Center

Coffee Shop

Rest Rooms

Annex and Domed Gardens:

Exit Rooms

Meditation Rooms

Rest Rooms

Medical Center

Counselors' Lounge and Pool

Escalators
Elevators
Stairs

3 Basement Levels—Garage, Utility Rooms, Storage

Staten Island

The Rational Death Woods, Gardens, and Greenhouse

Public Recreation Facilities (Pavilion, etc.)

Caretakers' Lodge

The Rational Death Archology

SCALE: 3/16" = 1'

FRONT ROOM
15' X 18'
(CLOSES TO
15' X 15')

ENTRANCE FROM
PUBLIC GARDEN

FIXED GLASS

FIXED GLASS

GLASS SLIDE DOORS

DRAPERY

LAMP TABLE

LOW TABLE

LAMP TABLE

DOUBLE-SIZE
CONVERTIBLE SOFA

LAMP TABLE

LAMP TABLE

W. C.

COUNSELOR'S ROOM

LAV.

ACCORDION DOORS

CLOSET

REFRIG. UNDER

SINK

COOK TOP

SHOWER

ENCLOSURE FOR TWO
36" X 84" WALL BEDS WHICH
SLIDE TO TWIN OR DOUBLE
BED POSITIONS

STORAGE WALL FOR
STACK CHAIRS, MATS,
PILLOWS, LINENS, ETC.

OUTER ROOM
11' X 14'
(CLOSES TO 11' X 11')

GLASS DOOR
EXIT INTO
PRIVATE GARDENS

GLASS SLIDE DOORS

GLASS SLIDE DOORS

DRAPERY

FIXED GLASS

FIXED GLASS

overload for accommodating two unrelated Exiters within the same suite.

Counselors are not required to live at Exit House, but they are welcome to do so. Resident Counselors, single or paired, will find each suite equipped for simple compact efficient living. (Initially not suitable for accommodating family life for children.) Resident Counselors may personalize their suites. Nonresident Counselors have identical suites assigned to them. There is less opportunity to personalize them since they must be shared on a rotation basis with another Counselor. Except in overload times, every effort is made to have no more than one Exiter accommodated in a suite at any given time. Since all assignments to Counselors, resident or not, are on a round-the-clock work schedule, the nonresidents are provided essentially the same facilities as the residents. The comfort of all Counselors is considered essential.

Each suite has two comfortably sized main rooms. The entry is from the Public Contemplation Garden into a "Front Room" developed to have a homelike, even cozy quality, although it has specific design elements which set limits upon such development. The room is warmed with carpeting, drapes, pictures and wall hangings, objets d'art, a book-lined wall, etc. Furniture is limited to a standard double-size convertible sofa bed, approximately six light-weight wicker and comfortable cushioned conversation chairs, four modular tables, and four table lamps. There is a telephone and radio and TV. Colors are neither vibrant nor somber. The emphasis of the room's mood is hospitable warmth. The room optionally may be widely opened into the Contemplation Garden or it may be made partially or totally private through the use of wooden louvers or drapes drawn across the all-glass facade.

The other main room is referred to as the "Outer Room."

Essentially it is a room that is bare except for the view. One completely glass wall gives onto the private Good Earth Gardens. There is no ceiling other than the dome of the Gardens. Despite this unusual openness, the Outer Room is comfortable for use as a sleeping room because the entire domed garden area is moisture- and temperature-controlled. Drapes and wooden louvers provide privacy from persons in the Gardens when desired. Two wall beds, each 42″ × 84″, easily fold out from the wall and slide into twin-bed positions or combine into a double bed. The Outer Room has a sizable storage wall which is partially available for Exiter's temporary storage as well as for general storage of extra chairs, linens, supplies. Natural light is controlled by wooden louvers overhead and on the window wall. Also, there is electrical illumination.

Between the two rooms is a private soundproof room for Counselor use only. It contains a built-in counter suitable for desk work or for dining by two, a compact two-burner kitchen unit with sink and refrigerator, and a clothes closet. The Counselor's Front Room and Outer Room each has access to bathroom facilities. The Front and Outer Rooms can be used in relationship to or independent of one another. Such passage and use flexibility is enabled by the various doors which can compartmentalize any room with or without obstructing access to other spaces. Movement and locking of doors can be done manually or via electric controls in the Counselor's Room.

Throughout, care is taken to avoid any atmosphere or decorative quality remindful of old-fashioned funeral parlors or traditional ceremonial spaces. The emphasis is not on separation from life. The emphasis is always on death as part of a recycling, earth-enriching, ongoing process. Death as an affirmation of life.

Plants and flowers spread from the gardens into the interiors, but only casually—no formal arrangements.

CLOTHING AT EXIT HOUSE

The only staff persons required to wear particular clothes whenever they are on duty are the Caretakers (Gardener-Guides). The men and women Caretakers roam the entire Exit House premises, inside and out—gardening, guiding, generally taking care of the place and providing general information and simple assistance to public and staff. Their uniforms are unobtrusive and yet readily distinguished. They wear footed sweat pants and tunics of earth browns, grays, and greens.

Optional clothing is provided for Exiters, visitors, and Counselors. For them, there is a wide variety of styles available in assorted selected colors—some bright, others muted. The garments are well-styled knits, loosely fitting and designed to provide maximum comfort, particularly for persons engaged in vigils. Counselors wear armbands at all times on duty, regardless of their attire.

An exception to the above is that all persons entering the private Good Earth Gardens (outside the Outer Rooms) must be attired in one of the above garments or in one of the slipover or wraparound togas provided for persons allowed in that area.

EXIT HOUSE CARETAKERS AND GROUNDS

These are uniquely important elements of the environment.

A vast dome encloses all of the Exit House annex and

gardens at their city headquarters. The enclosed space is temperature- and moisture-controlled. There are exceptionally beautiful lawns and shrubs and blooming flowers and trees. Small safe animals such as chipmunks and squirrels go about their business of living and dying. Water falls here, ripples or babbles there, and adds its sounds to the chirping and song of colorful birds. Human voices mingle with these natural sounds. Children's laughter and cries, argumentative tones, soothing sounds, soft weeping, an anguished wail, whispers, are all heard and yet—as they blend into the other natural sounds—are absorbed. There are essentially no regulating or prohibiting signs. One is free to wander anywhere, along one of the few paths, or off them. One may sit alone under a tree or lie on the luxurious lawn or gather with others in a secluded natural alcove. There are secluded spots but no closed spots, yet there is always privacy. Almost everywhere in sight one can see a Caretaker quietly tending the garden—its soil, its grass, flowers, shrubs, and trees; its fountains and falls and brooks; its sculptures; its people—planting, enriching, pruning, recycling, ever sensitive to the needs of the earth and its creatures. Always at hand to guide and help everyone near. Green- and brown-clad men and women who care.

A bereaved man sits weeping on the bench. Nearby a Caretaker is on her knees turning compost into a garden bed. Two children come running merrily into the scene. The Caretaker continues her gardening but is mindful of what is happening. Is there a sign that the man feels disturbed by the children? Or that he is oblivious? Or that the children's sounds are renewing sounds for him? Perhaps the Caretaker will just keep gardening. Or maybe she will guide the children to the "climbing rock just beyond the red tree over there."

Anyone who cares may undergo training for Caretaking at Exit House.

EXIT HOUSE: WHERE YOU MAY TERMINATE YOUR LIFE WITHOUT PAIN, WITH DIGNITY AND RESPONSIBILITY

The decision to end one's conscious life is a solemn one. Until the establishment of Exit House it usually was fraught with anguish. The grim fearful questions of suicide—of how and where, coupled with feelings such as guilt—so preoccupied the mind of the Self-Terminator that there was little opportunity for dwelling on aspects of life which might enable one to die peacefully, even joyfully.

Do you know the blissful feeling of lying down to sleep after long work? Maybe you didn't accomplish as much as you wished or as someone else might have, but you had worked. You made mistakes and the results weren't the best in the world, but then they weren't the worst, either. You had done what you felt up to doing and there was satisfaction in that. You felt exhaustion all through you. And the good sweet feeling of slipping into sleep. If the time came when the exhaustion was no longer relieved by sleep and you felt it too difficult to go on, might not you find sweetness in the possibility of slipping gently into death? The Exit House staff believes you might and that you have the right to choose the time.

But suppose you get to thinking of how others would feel about your death. You feel awful thinking of someone suffering? From those feelings, perhaps the Exit House Counselor could help you draw words of comfort into a letter.

If you don't feel like thinking through all sorts of ties

you have—the bills to be paid, unfinished business, things being abandoned—perhaps the Exit House Counselor could help you untangle matters and put your mind to rest.

You feel worthless? If you don't want to go on feeling that way, if you'd rather feel yourself to be of value, perhaps an Exit House Counselor could help you know how you can make even your last moments count.

Exit House Counselors respect your right to determine your life's fullness and length. They appreciate the solemnity of Self-Termination. They believe there can be goodness, dignity, peace, and beauty in dying, and they are trained to help people know such moments.

PREPARATION FOR LAST MOMENTS

Determining the moment of your death is your right. Our wish is to help you plan responsibly and to enable you a dignified recycling of yourself. Following are a number of random thoughts and questions which it might be helpful for us to consider together. They are based on the assumption that your time of recycling has been settled in your mind.

Who are the people most likely to be affected by or to notice your death? Which of them do you care about? Which care about you? Which do you love or like, or dislike?

Do you wish your relationship with any of these significant persons had been different? What would you have preferred? Would you feel better about yourself if they understood your wishes? If so, we'd like to help you prepare such notes for delivery to them. If you like, we will help them understand your feelings.

Are you abandoning any of your belongings? Would

you feel better if you could control what becomes of them? We can help you do that. Have you left a will, arranged for the disposition of your estate (i.e., personal belongings and property) regardless of how small, humble, extensive, or valuable? Will anyone be burdened by handling your estate? Who? Would you like yourself better if you could spare them the responsibility? We can help you do that.

Together, can we make a reasonable estimate of how long it would take to accomplish these things? Would the moment of your recycling have to be postponed if we undertook adjustments? If so, would you prefer that we make a condensed plan which would assure recycling within the next twelve hours, or would you like to postpone that moment while we carry out the fuller adjustments?

We would like to help you make distribution of your estate in a way which would make you feel best about yourself. You have at least four alternatives. One is to specify in writing (i.e., make a bona fide will) that certain belongings are to become the property of certain other persons or organizations. Second, you may simply abandon belongings, in which event the New York City Public Administrator will routinely handle a liquidation at a public auction. Proceeds are then held for one year against claims by kin and creditors. Unclaimed moneys become government property. Third, you may assign belongings to Exit House for liquidation and channeling into the Exit House Foundation, which in turn directs all such bequests and donations into the Exit House programs which have made our service available to you and which will help determine the availability of improved Exiting service to others. Fourth, the foregoing alternatives can be combined. Exit House is equipped to assist your choice.

We can help you estimate the cost of estate handling and, if you wish, help you plan coverage of such expenses.

There are limited funds available for estate processing in the event one's estate cannot meet the expenses.

Have you an inventory? We could help you prepare one. Do you know the value of your property? We can provide assessment. Would you like to liquidate your estate prior to death? We can make this possible. Would you like to designate sentimental mementos?

Consider the last moments before recycling. Would you like any person or persons to be with you? Who? Why?

Does it matter to you where you die? Arrangements can be made for you to die away from Exit House in some instances. Consider what your alternatives are and what difference, if any, your selection would make to how you feel about yourself. We want to help your last moments be as you would like them to be.

Would you feel better in these moments if, in advance, you considered how you might appear in death? And determined, yourself, how that would be?

The Exit House philosophy is such that we hope your last moments will be enhanced with the knowledge that after you are dead the recycling of your body will begin immediately to be of value, whether through your having the responsibility of directing it to scientific use in research and/or transplantation; by burial of your enriching body in the earth without application of any materials which might delay the time of the earth's reclamation; or by cremation, transposing your body into earth-enriching fertilizer. If, on the other hand, more traditional arrangements have been made for your body, Exit House wishes to help. You can be helped to arrange any lawful disposition of your body which suits you or those interested in you.

Are there religious considerations which would enhance your final moments?

Are there requests you'd like to make of Exit House?

Anything you'd like us to do before or after your death which would enhance your final moments or hours?

Would you like to help create or to examine your Exit House file before you die? Would you like to add anything to it? Documents from your past? Photographs in addition to the official Exit House photographs? Requests? Bequests? Instructions? Copies of letters, current or past? A statement about your experience at Exit House? Do you want any part of your file to be held confidential for any specified period of time, not to exceed fifty years?

Consider the various methods available to you for life termination. Have you a preference? Would it help to discuss your alternatives?

Have you any recommendations to make to other Exiters? To your government? To Exit House?

EXIT HOUSE BENEFITS

1. Opportunity for an individual to avail self of painless dignified Self-Termination or Euthanasia.

2. Opportunity for a Self-Termination to provide heirs with fullest estate rights via Self-Termination Certification.

3. Opportunity to involve interested persons in planning.

4. Opportunity to contribute to research on the Self-Termination condition and to basic life research.

OPTIONAL PLACES OF TERMINATION

At Exit House: Facilities previously described are available to all qualified persons who wish to use them. A wide variety of reasons exist for selecting Exit House as the place to die. A unique reason is that it enables Exiters to completely settle their affairs in advance of death (disposing of living quarters, etc.). Additional reasons include the more direct access to facilities and the tendency for speedier decision-making due to fewer distractions.

At Home: A common reason for electing to terminate one's life at home is the wish to spend one's last moments in a familiar surrounding, sometimes with relatives or friends in attendance. Sometimes the home of a friend is selected. While terminations at home are acceptable to Exit House and sometimes recommended, they are not routinely encouraged due to the extra time required of staff.

Other: Sometimes Counselors are called to hospitals or accident scenes. The Exit House Emergency Team usually handles the latter situation.

DISPOSITION OF EXITERS' BELONGINGS

Whenever possible, Exiters are asked to clarify the disposition of their belongings before termination; if possible, confirmation by designated persons is sought. If the Exiter doesn't arrange disposition on her or his own (with or without Exit House assistance), she or he is informed that property may be assigned to Exit House; otherwise, it will be turned over to the New York City Public Administrator for public auction.

In the event disposition is assigned to Exit House, a Caretaker is dispatched to the Exiter's residence to make an inventory. The latter is turned over to the Exit House Legal Department for processing.

When indicated, Exit House may place an Exiter's possessions in storage through the processing period.

WHO IS ELIGIBLE FOR CERTIFIED SELF-TERMINATION?

Only bona fide residents of New York City (until laws are changed so Exit Houses may be established throughout the country) eighteen years of age or older.

Any of the above who are able to participate in the Service and Research Process at Exit House.

Persons must be able to communicate their desires (themselves or via appointed guardians).

Persons must be able to administer the selected means of exit of their own accord.

Any person meeting the above qualifications is eligible, and may not be denied Exit House benefits.

Above persons unable to participate *at* Exit House may be determined to be eligible for the Exit House Home Service or the Exit House Emergency Service.

WHO IS ELIGIBLE FOR CERTIFIED SELF-TERMINATION BY EUTHANASIA?

Only persons who are bona fide residents of New York City and forty years of age or older.

Above persons who desire to die and are able to participate with an Exit House Counselor in the decision considerations but who, for any reason, are physically or emotionally unable to administer their own self-termination. Such persons may have an Exit Means administered to them by a licensed Exit House Euthanasist Counselor.

If indicated, above persons may receive Exit House service at their own location via the Exit House Emergency or Home Service.

Any person meeting the above qualifications is eligible and entitled to benefits identical to those of Self-Terminators, and may not be denied Exit House benefits.

EXIT HOUSE CATCHMENT AREA AND RESIDENCY REQUIREMENTS

The catchment area for Exit House is New York City. Applicants for admissions to Exit House must have a current New York City Residency Card.

SERVICES AVAILABLE TO PERSONS NOT ELIGIBLE FOR TERMINATION VIA EXIT HOUSE

Non–New York City residents, people under the age of eighteen, and those unable to participate in the Exit House process are currently ineligible for the benefits of Exit House certification or for access to Exit Means. However, a limited service is available to everyone interested in Self-Termination or Euthanasia.

The Exit House Social Service Department will provide a Counselor to provide much the same services that are available to eligible applicants, except that Counselors are legally prohibited from providing Exit Means and they cannot provide the same guarantees of estate rights which are available to eligible persons. They will help an applicant to know his rights, to weigh his decision, to make preparations for himself and his heirs in the event he determines to terminate his life without certification, and he will be given an opportunity to participate in Exit House research. For such persons the Social Service Department provides short-term counseling and a full referral service.

The Social Service Department also provides counseling for persons involved with Self-Termination or potential Self-Terminators, certified or not.

EXIT HOUSE HOME SERVICE

Exit House is equipped to make its services available to qualified persons away from the Exit House premises under various circumstances, particularly for persons who are not ambulatory and for persons who have completed the Exit House process but prefer to terminate their lives in familiar surroundings.

EXIT HOUSE EMERGENCY SERVICE

Exit House has an Emergency Team trained to handle crisis situations outside the Exit House grounds (but within the catchment area) and equipped with the best standard ambulance facilities.

The Team is comprised of a counselor, a medic, an assistant, and a driver. All four are specially trained at Exit House. Aside from being skilled in traditional life-saving procedures, they are particularly trained in the assessment of Self-Termination decision-making; to focus upon determining the Self-Terminator's wishes in relationship to his potential survivors but separate from their wishes; to make the Self-Terminator as physically comfortable as possible while, simultaneously, assisting the Self-Terminator in making the most thoughtful preparation for death and its consequences to survivors; to collect relevant material for survivors, the Legal Commission, and research. The counselor is a licensed Euthanasist.

THE EXIT HOUSE FOUNDATION

This branch of Exit House is responsible for distribution of all funds incoming from bequests and donations. Its basic administrative costs are carried by the federal government. While most funds are recycled into the various aspects of the Exit House program—Research, Library, and Training—the Foundation also provides grants to support other relevant undertakings.

THE EXIT HOUSE RESEARCH
FOUNDATION AND LIBRARY

The Foundation is federally established for the sole purpose of researching the experimental Exit House program. It has no control over Exit House. Its responsibility is to study all Exit House data and report findings to the government and to Exit House and to make the findings available to the general public. It may, of course, make recommendations. Exit House is to comply with its requests for cooperative procedures providing Exit House decides it can incorporate same without undue interference with Exit House goals.

In compliance with the wishes of the Foundation, Exit House prepares a file for each Self-Terminator. Most files will not exceed booklet or book size. Some files will require boxing. Shelf-size standardized binders, envelopes, and boxes are provided for each Self-Terminator. Larger items of such relevance to the Foundation research as to call for storage will be held in the Foundation's warehouse as long as it is deemed appropriate. The latter items may

be disposed of as per the Foundation's wishes, unless the
Self-Terminator provides other arrangements.

Nonprofessional access to Self-Terminator files is acceptable to Exit House Foundation under the standard
library procedures of control. The Self-Terminator may,
however, elect to limit access to his file to professional
researchers. The Self-Terminator may also designate portions of his file as confidential for a proscribed period of
time, not to exceed fifty years, preferably less. Such confidential files will be sealed and removed from even
scholastic access until the designated time-release.

THE RATIONAL DEATH LEGAL DEPARTMENT

When the federal government was establishing Exit
House, it recognized that many unique legal considerations would arise from all directions. Much law existed
reflecting the lack of recognition of an individual's right
to Self-Termination or clearly denying such a right. Property rights commonly were given legal priority over an
individual's life-death rights. Under such circumstances
it was evident that Exit House would not be able to recruit
staff, nor would Exit House be able to function without
constant jeopardy from litigation. Federal law was therefore revised accordingly. New York State and New York
City necessarily had to comply.

By federal law, all certified Exit House Self-Termina-
tions are to be regarded in the eyes of the law precisely as
though a death by natural causes had occurred.

The Rational Death Legal Department's federally
funded staff is enormous, as are its responsibilities. They
are to assure that the Exit House staff is adequately protected from protesters and prosecutions. No staff member

can be prosecuted for homicide except for actions taken outside of the line of duty. The Rational Death Legal Department's staff carries responsibility to assure that the estate rights of the Self-Terminator's beneficiaries will be respected. Further, they are to handle any other legal matters related to Exit House and the public's reactions. They cannot establish policy for Exit House but have the responsibility of advising and recommending. Also, they are responsible for providing guiding consultation to federal, state, and city legislators.

INSURANCE DIVISION OF THE RATIONAL DEATH LEGAL DEPARTMENT

Major litigation focused on insurance. Suicide clauses in existing insurance policies of New York City residents have been automatically invalidated. New applicants for insurance had to be protected against increased insurance costs, so insurance companies are forbidden to raise their rates in relation to Self-Termination before five years, and then they can do so only if they can demonstrate, with actual figures, the necessity. To protect the insurance companies against abuse, new applicants' policies may have a Self-Termination limitation clause for a period no longer than three years. (Interestingly, some companies have not taken advantage of this at all, and some inserted Self-Termination clauses which designated limitations for less than three years.) All insurance companies are now required by the Internal Revenue Service to provide new data on insurance for Self-Terminators. Insurance companies everywhere, seeing the handwriting on the wall, are developing new formulations. Some initially anticipated that at the end of the initial five years, companies would suffer severe losses or would be in danger of severe losses due to legalized Self-Termination. Most are more sanguine now and anticipate that very little adjustment in premiums will become necessary—that even with some increase in the Self-Termination rate, there will be a leveling off. All new policies carrying a Self-Termination limitation clause are required to carry also a Euthanasia clause, invalidating any limitation to beneficiaries of persons dying by certified Euthanasia.

PHOTOGRAPHS AND AUTHORIZATIONS

Each Exiter's file must contain at least one photograph taken by Exit House photographer, either before or after termination. This is particularly essential for the records due to the fact that sometimes there can be little if any opportunity to verify the Exiter's identification. Other photographs may be filed, but an official Exit House photograph is required also.

A copy of the official Exit House photograph must be attached to the Exiter's signed authorization(s) for Exit House to participate in termination and, when appropriate, for Exit House to handle various matters in estate settling.

EXIT HOUSE CERTIFICATION

Exit House certification is presently the only Certification of Self-Termination which, by federal law, guarantees to heirs the estate rights identical with the fullest rights recognized for persons who die of any natural or accidental cause.

TERMINATING METHODS

An Exiter capable of arriving at her or his own decision and capable of self-administration may choose to ingest an Exit Pill or Exit Liquid. An Exit Injection and Exit Vapor Inhalation are also available. These Exit Medications are strictly regulated and made available only under the supervision of a Counselor.

Any of the above four methods of termination are available for regulated use by Euthanasia Exiters, some of whom are essentially Self-Terminators in that they are consciously able to make their own decisions. They differ in that they are unable to self-administer, and therefore require the service of a Euthanasist. Euthanasia Exiters unable to make their own decisions are terminated by use of Exit Vapor or Injection.

All methods are exceedingly swift and physically painless—except, of course, for the momentary discomfort which accompanies any injection.

BODY DISPOSITION/RECYCLING

Whenever possible, the Exiter's wishes are determined and carried out. If an Exiter had no preference as to body disposition/recycling, relatives or friends may make the determination. If latter are in conflict, then Exit House will make the determination. Disposition may be made apart from Exit House and in any way the Exiter and/or interested persons arrange. Otherwise Exit House will handle bodies as follows:

Exit House's goal of helping people to make fullest use

of themselves for the benefit of the earth—including humankind—is reflected in the alternative methods it offers Exiters for disposition of their bodies, in addition to services offered elsewhere.

Burial on Exit House Grounds: Caretakers remove bodies to Rational Death Woods, the forested acreage owned and maintained by Exit House on Staten Island. There, with reverence for the earth, without embalming or enclosures, and without ceremony, the Caretakers bury the bodily remains to decompose and enrich the earth in the most natural way. The enriched loam of the forest is recycled to the Exit House Gardens. The Rational Death Woods is a beautiful place where the land is revered and made useful and available to the public. No graves are marked, or held for nonuse or as individual property. An exceptionally lush place, the Woods serve the public well. Initially persons fearful of death felt some reluctance to visit the Woods, but as others discovered its beauty it has become popular as a life space for play as well as contemplation. In the spring its flowers are abundant in open areas. For those who like to pick flowers, the Caretakers will show which flowers may be picked. Other flowers are gathered by the Caretakers and made available to the public at a flower and plant stand.

Cremation: In the New York City crematoriums. All ash from Exiters is used in fertilization of the earth unless the Exiter requests otherwise.

Recycling of Bodies through Science: Unless an Exiter designates otherwise, all bodies are made available to bona fide scientific institutions for purposes of research and/or transplantations.

When an Exiter is pronounced dead, recycling begins instantly. Caretakers tend the body for the next hours. The length of their care varies from one situation to another, but usually does not exceed twenty-four hours. Usually bodies are removed from the Exit Rooms. Wrapped in a simple cotton sheet to facilitate handling, bodies are carried into the private Exit House Gardens, where each body is laid in a secluded place on the ground. Caretakers guide relatives, friends, and interested persons to their Exiter. The bodies of Exiters remain on the ground of the Exit House private gardens until they are removed by the Exit House van to the Rational Death Woods.

RELIGION

Exit House makes no provision for religious ceremony. Exiters may, however, be assisted in making arrangements for religious consultation as part of their Exiting preparation. Counselors will help Exiters arrange for religious ceremonies off the Exit House premises. If conflict exists between Exiter's wishes and those of family and friends, Exit House will bring about adjustment where possible, and otherwise will support the specified wish of the Exiter.

Caretakers and Guides are trained not to impose their own religious views upon Exiters.

PUBLIC ACCESS

The public is invited to visit the grounds daily from dawn until dusk. Tours of the buildings are available daily from 12:00 noon until 5:00 P.M. A reception area for applicants, family, and friends is open at all hours.